feeding baby

everyday recipes for healthy infants and toddlers

# feeding baby

JOACHIM SPLICHAL
& CHRISTINE SPLICHAL
*with Pamela Mosher*

Food photography by
VICTORIA PEARSON

CELESTIAL ARTS
Berkeley | Toronto

Copyright © 2003, 2008 by Joachim Splichal and
    Christine Splichal
Food photography copyright © 2002 by Victoria Pearson

Celestial Arts
an imprint of Ten Speed Press
PO Box 7123
Berkeley, California 94707
www.tenspeed.com

Distributed in Australia by Simon & Schuster Australia, in
Canada by Ten Speed Press Canada, in New Zealand by
Southern Publishers Group, in South Africa by Real Books,
and in the United Kingdom and Europe by Publishers
Group UK.

Cover and text design by Toni Tajima

Photos on pages x and 3 by Sam Nicholson and Dianna
Olivia Day. Our thanks to Neiman Marcus Beverly Hills
for providing props for photography. On page 79, ceramic
plates by Christiane Perrochon exclusively for Neiman
Marcus. On page 106, bib by Neiman Marcus.

The Library of Congress has cataloged the hardcover
edition as follows:
Splichal, Joachim.
Feeding Baby : simple healthy recipes for babies and their
families / Joachim Splichal and Christine Splichal.
       p. cm.
Includes bibliographical references and index.
ISBN 1-58008-500-8
1. Infants (Newborn)—Nutrition. 2. Infants—Nutrition.
3. Toddlers—Nutrition. 4. Cookery (Baby foods) I. Splichal,
Christine. II. Title.
RJ216.S657 2003
613.2'083'2—dc21

ISBN-13: 978-1-58761-317-3

ISBN-10: 1-58761-317-4

Printed in China
First printing this edition, 2008

1 2 3 4 5 6 7 8 9 10 — 12 11 10 09 08

For our twins, Nicolas and Stephane,
who inspired us to rediscover the pleasures of
honest, simple foods.

# contents

# acknowledgments

We would like to thank the dedicated and talented crew that brought this book to completion. Our gratitude goes to the team at Ten Speed Press and Celestial Arts, who enthusiastically embraced the project; editor Lisa Westmoreland, who shepherded the book to press with a discerning eye; Brigit Binns, who consulted with us early on in the project and got us focused; Camille Renk, who thoroughly tested the recipes; Pamela Mosher, who worked with us to write the recipes and recount our experiences; pediatric dietitian Gail Seche, whose expertise was invaluable; photographer Victoria Pearson, who can turn a dish of carrot purée into a candidate for the cover of *Gourmet* (and probably has done so at some point); stylist Ann Johnstad, who seems to know intuitively how objects can tell stories; and designer Toni Tajima, who brought it all so brilliantly to the page. And we are very grateful to Sam Nicholson and Diana Oliva Day for their wonderful, candid photos of our family. Finally, we would like to thank Christine's father, André Mandion, for his inspiration and wise advice.

# introduction

When our twins were born, people often asked us how we managed to find the time to start our babies off eating freshly prepared food instead of conventional bottled baby food. The truth is that it wasn't a huge ordeal for us; it was simply a natural progression because of who we are and the role food plays in our lives. We started giving our boys "real" food—purées and mashed, steamed vegetables—at about four months. By the time they were eleven months old, we'd all have something like sweet potato risotto, pink lentils with peaches, or Napa cabbage with lemon and bacon for dinner. We adults might add a piece of fish or meat to round out our own menu, but everyone sat at the same table and ate the same food together—simple, fresh, honest, and, above all, nutritious food. Just because we run "gourmet" restaurants doesn't mean we feed our kids "gourmet" food. If they want to eat gourmet food, that's something they can decide later.

This is not a revolutionary concept. In fact, it's quite old-fashioned. Before the industrialization of food preparation, everyone had to make meals from scratch for their babies. The advent of canning and bottling was a quantum leap forward, and when bottled baby food became available, it must have seemed like modern, time-saving progress at its best. Because we are creatures of habit, the common approach for many years now has been to just "go with the flow" and serve bottled baby food. But we feel something important has been lost. It's not just the vitamins and minerals that are destroyed when fresh food is bottled and heat-treated to improve shelf life, it's the warm feeling that comes from sitting around the table and "breaking bread" together as a family. We believe that the practice of feeding baby processed food has contributed to the practice of members of the family eating different foods at different times, even when the children are older. Surely this is not good for the nuclear family.

## MY DAD

My father, André Mandion, is a pâtissier, a pastry chef, well known in the southwest region of France, near Biarritz. He is a strong advocate of unprocessed food. No cooking would be his choice; the less done to the food, the better. He taught me to steam instead of boil and to use only what was fresh and in season. —**C.S.**

There is a tendency in these busy times to rely on prepared foods for meals. Just take a stroll through a supermarket and see how many baskets are full of packaged, premade meals, and how few fresh vegetables are in those same baskets. Real food is a wonderful thing! The crunch of a fresh carrot, the briny smell of a freshly caught fish, the snap of crisp green beans . . . we have a responsibility to our children to promote the practice of eating real, fresh food, prepared the old-fashioned way, with our hands. If we can familiarize our children now with the tastes and textures of real food as opposed to processed, prepared food, then we are sending them on a healthy, happy road to adulthood and all the myriad pleasures of food.

And it's important to remember that food comes from the earth, not from a plastic box or bag. There's nothing wrong with seeing a little dirt on our food, and that's why we love the farmers' markets springing up all over the country. They're good for the consumers and good for the farmers. Let's make sure these markets and the choice of fresh vegetables in our supermarkets remain available until our children grow up. We're all aware of the importance of fresh food, and we doubt that most adults would want to live on a diet of canned foods. So why should we expect it of our children?

Our kids are eleven years old now, and it's very gratifying for us as parents to see the results of our endeavors. An example we saw very early on was during the holiday season several years ago. At Christmas the kids had exactly what we had—not the whole multicourse meal, of course, but one or two parts of it. Nicolas even said to the cook, "Very good, très bon!" He was two and a half! We were proud parents. We went to visit friends for Thanksgiving and the other kids at the table refused to eat most of the food, but our boys were game for everything. All we had to do was cut it up.

We can now give them just about any food, and 99 percent of the time they have what we're having. They aren't likely to turn their noses up at foods that aren't familiar, because almost everything is familiar. For instance, for lunch we might all have braised pork with apricots and onions—we just cut theirs up and have ours whole. The next day we might have lamb stew with carrots and prunes, or tuna with roasted garlic and tomatoes. It's all fresh, healthy food, and it's not scary to the kids. Of course, there are exceptions. For some reason, they don't like Brussels sprouts. But we know many adults who don't like Brussels sprouts, either. In writing this book, we are hoping to share our strategies, trials, and successes with a wider audience.

Of course, everyone wants the very best for their babies; there's no question about that. But we're all busy people, and most of us don't have help at home. Preparing food from scratch for baby might, at first, sound like a lot of trouble. Far from it! If you have a steamer basket, almost any vegetable can be steamed in 3 to 8 minutes (after the water boils). For the first few months after breast-feeding stops, you'll have to throw it in the blender, but after that you'll only have to chop it up a little. After a few months of puréeing, the kids can eat exactly what the rest of the family eats, with a few exceptions. Instead of being more trouble, it's actually less. If the grown-ups are having lamb chops for supper, make up a batch of white beans with parsley and garlic. For the kids it makes a healthy main course, for you a tasty side dish. There is also a cost benefit.

**DEVELOPING TASTES**

Although they are fraternal twins and began life eating exactly the same things, Nicolas loves Brie and Camembert, but Stephane hates it. Nicolas also loves mustard and pickles. There are always going to be differences in taste. **—C.S.**

## DINING EN FAMILLE

Europeans are very traditional about mealtimes. Everyone sits down to eat together, whoever is there— the nanny, the au pair, a friend. The ritual is always the same, even though the participants may change. And there is no TV in the kitchen or dining room. **—C.S.**

## PICKY EATERS

Kids can be picky eaters, and it's a great temptation to give them pasta when the meal you've prepared is rejected and you can't think of anything else. Pasta is actually very low in nutrients, so we only gave our boys pasta about once every two weeks, unless there was a little in the soup. The same goes

Bottled baby foods are expensive, and often the full bottle doesn't get used. Sharing the same food among the whole family means less expense and less waste.

Most important, it's healthy food. Kids, not just here in the States but in other parts of the world as well, tend to eat unhealthy food. They start out with bland, soft food and then don't want to explore beyond those flavors and textures. How many times have you heard kids yelling for pizza instead of what the adults are having? And it's not even real pizza! It's bland topping on soft dough with too much cheese, washed down with sugary soda. They develop bad habits and continue them into adolescence and young adulthood, often resulting in problems with obesity and poor health. We decided early on that sweetened sodas never would be found in our refrigerator. They are full of sugar, and a sure recipe for dental problems. Fruit juice and water are the only beverages on the menu.

If you make your children aware from an early age that there is something else besides bland, fatty fast food, they will develop a palate and always be open to new tastes. And another important point: when it comes to vitamins and nutrients, there is simply no comparison between bottled food and freshly made food. Prepared baby foods and juices can be full of sugar and preservatives. By making your own baby food, you'll know exactly what is going into it. This was a huge motivation for us in starting our kids off on fresh food, and we believe it will be a strong motivation for many other parents as well.

There is, of course, a science to the practice of good nutrition. That's why we have pediatric dietician Gail Seche helping us to make this book nutritionally sound. When we began this project, we read lots of books on nutrition. Christine basically gave herself a miniature course on the subject. Also, her father is extremely involved with naturopathy in France, and we had his advice, too. If you do some research and arm yourself with some of the wonderful books available, you'll be able to make informed decisions about what to feed your baby, and when.

# Cautionary Advice

It is extremely important that, from the moment your baby begins to eat solids, her meals are always supervised. In addition to the bonding that takes place between baby and parent during feeding, it is important to watch for signs of allergic reaction and choking. The former will be of immediate concern, since the possibility of allergic reaction exists from the moment your baby ingests her first food other than breast milk. Choking, although always a concern, is more apt to occur when your baby progresses to food that is more chewy and textured. Since both an allergic reaction and choking require immediate response, your full attention should be focused on your baby during her meals.

### ALLERGIES

As you make the transition from breast-feeding to feeding your baby solids, you may find that your baby will have an allergic reaction to certain foods. An allergic reaction is caused by the immune system's reaction to what it perceives as a

for potatoes. As much as possible, we tried to stick with the original meal selection. If we had rushed to provide something else, we would have been sending the kids a message that says we'll keep trying until we find something acceptable. Remember the old adage: "Start out as you mean to go on." Few of us want to be juggling different foods, desperately trying to find something the kids will agree to eat, for the next eighteen years.

**—C.S.**

threat. When an ingested food is identified as a foreign body, the immune system overproduces antibodies to counteract it.

Signs of allergic reaction vary from hives, which are usually immediate, to diarrhea, nausea, vomiting, difficulty breathing, runny nose, swelling of the lips or face, itching, and shock. Symptoms can appear from within minutes to up to two hours. Watch your baby carefully, since it's easy to read an allergic reaction as a cold or other illness. Consult your pediatrician to verify any suspicions.

Theories vary widely on what causes allergies, but if there is a history of food allergies in your family, there is a chance that your baby will develop similar ones. Those chances are increased if both parents have food allergies. Neither of us has food allergies, and, fortunately, our boys never developed any, but we were definitely on the watch for allergic reactions.

Good basic means of allergy prevention are breast-feeding and delaying the introduction of solids until your baby is at least six months old.

The generally accepted method to determine which foods cause an allergic reaction is called the four-day wait rule. Allergic reactions are not always immediate; it can be several days before a reaction occurs. For this reason, it's advisable to wait approximately four days after introducing a new food to see whether an allergic reaction is triggered. Introduce the new food by itself, not mixed with anything else, in order to gauge its effect. During the waiting period, previously tested foods can be served but do not introduce any other new foods. Don't overdo it with the new food because too frequent feedings of a new food can create a sensitivity to it.

Known allergens are the ones to watch, especially if there is a family history. Among these are cow's milk, soy, egg white, wheat, peanuts and possibly other nuts, shellfish, pork, corn, and strawberries. Some allergies will decline as your baby gets older, and some, especially allergies to eggs, cow's milk, wheat, and shellfish, will remain throughout life.

In the case of cow's milk, a distinction should be made between an allergic reaction and lactose intolerance, which doesn't involve the immune system. Lactase is the enzyme that breaks down milk sugar, lactose, in the intestines. If your baby's intestines lack the enzyme, the lactose is not digested and bacteria develop, causing gas, abdominal pain, and diarrhea. Symptoms can occur within thirty minutes to up to two hours.

## CHOKING

In general, the risk of choking is greatest for children under three years of age, although older children are susceptible as well. Small, hard objects are usually the culprits. Among these are popcorn, berries, raisins, nut pieces, hard candy, seeds, and hard pieces of fruit or vegetables—in short, anything that is hard, small enough to fit in your child's mouth, and large enough to become lodged in his throat or windpipe.

In addition to being watchful, you can take other precautions. Cut up the food into pieces small enough that they can be swallowed and not lodge in your child's throat. Never let your child eat while he is lying down or walking around. Make sure that breads or biscuits, such as teething biscuits, are either too hard for a piece to break off or soft enough to dissolve when put into your child's mouth.

You'll know your child is choking if she has difficulty breathing, her arms are flailing, she can't cough up the blockage, or she is starting to turn blue. Be extremely cautious about trying to manually remove the stuck object; you could push it in further and worsen the situation. Call for emergency medical help immediately. If you are not already trained in CPR, it is a good idea to take one of the classes offered by your local Red Cross chapter or hospital.

## A WORD ABOUT SALT

Resist adding salt to your baby's food until they are over two years old. Your baby will easily get the required daily amount of sodium from his normal diet. Since many of the recipes in the book are also intended for adults, they contain salt. The majority of these are in the Meals chapter, for children two to three years old, and Family Feasts, for the entire family. However, salt can be eliminated or reduced when preparing any of these recipes for your baby. Since she hasn't developed a taste for salt, she won't find the food prepared from these recipes bland. Conversely, many of the recipes for children younger than two are also suitable for older children and adults. Salt can be added to make these recipes palatable for them.

# How to Use This Book

The recipes offered here are adaptable. Some are intended for babies and some for grown-ups, but we like to think they'll be used for both because that's the way we do it at our house. You won't feed baby everything you eat, but baby's food can easily play a big role in your own menu. In fact, you'll probably eat more nutritious food than usual if you eat the same food you prepare for baby. In the summer, make Salmon with Couscous (page 78) for baby's lunch—but make enough so it's a ready-made dinner for the rest of the family. The result: baby has had protein for lunch, and you have made yourself an easy, delicious dinner.

Or, steam some broccoli and cauliflower, then toss half or three-quarters of it with some salad greens and vinaigrette for your own lunch. Save the rest for baby's dinner, and all that's left to do is chop and serve. The combinations are endless, and your own creativity is bound to come into play. The best part is that you and your baby are both eating fresh, flavorful food full of vitamins and minerals and without added sugar or preservatives. Plus, you are nurturing a young soul toward a lifetime of adventurous, healthy eating and civilized dining.

# getting started

The first step when approaching a new recipe is to read it all the way through before you begin. This will enable you to assemble the necessary ingredients so that they are ready for use. You can also devise your strategy, especially if you are preparing a meal with several dishes or courses.

## Basic Techniques

The recipes in this book do not reflect the haute cuisine that I am known for at Patina, but many of the techniques are identical to those used in the restaurant's kitchen, and they are simple. Blanching and refreshing are standard procedures for preparing green vegetables and some fruits, whether I'm cooking at the restaurant or in my kitchen. Braising is a traditional method that makes the most of a large piece of meat, and deglazing is essential to create the delicious sauce. A very useful technique to master, caramelizing adds a delicate sweet, slightly burnt flavor to onions, apples, and most famously crème brûlée and crème caramel. Freezing and reheating are simple, logical procedures that you will become an expert at during your first months of parenthood.

### BLANCHING AND REFRESHING

Blanching preserves the flavor, texture, and color of vegetables, and some fruits, and prepares them for further cooking. Fill a large bowl with ice water. Bring to a boil a pot of water that is large enough for the amount of vegetables being prepared. Drop the vegetables gently into the pot and cook, uncovered, until they're brightly colored, usually 2 to 3 minutes, or whatever is recommended in the recipe. Remove them immediately with a slotted spoon and plunge into the bowl of ice water, which stops the cooking. This practice is also known as refreshing the vegetables. Once drained, the vegetables are ready to be sautéed, puréed, or, in the case of tomatoes or thin-skinned fruit, peeled.

## BRAISING

Braising is a wonderful method of preparing large cuts of meat, usually pot roasts or veal shanks, that produces tender, flavorful results. Heat olive oil in a large Dutch oven, sear the meat on all sides, season with salt and pepper, add vegetables and stock—whatever the recipe calls for—and then cover tightly and place in the oven or leave on the stovetop over low heat to simmer, according to the recipe. A delicious crust will form on the meat, and it will be so tender it will almost fall off the bone, if there is a bone involved.

## DEGLAZING

Deglazing is generally the first step in preparing a sauce. To a pan in which meat has been seared, add liquid—veal stock, wine, cream, lemon juice, or vegetable broth—and heat while scraping up the browned bits of meat with a wooden spoon. Continue cooking and stirring until the liquid is reduced and thickened, or use the liquid as the base for a sauce.

## CARAMELIZING

Sugar is the principal agent in the caramelizing process. Sugar is dissolved in water and heated, as the pan is swirled, until it turns into a golden brown—or caramel—colored syrup. Apples and onions can be caramelized by sprinkling them with sugar and sautéing them in butter or oil until a golden brown glaze forms.

## FREEZING, THAWING, AND REHEATING BABY FOOD

Most of the foods that you prepare for your baby can be safely stored in the refrigerator, covered tightly, for 1 day. It is best to use a heatproof microwave dish that you can either pop in the microwave or set in a small pan partially filled with boiling water to heat. Tepid food is a breeding ground for bacteria, so always reheat the food until it is hot—about 165°F for 2 minutes—and don't reheat it more than once. Stir it thoroughly and taste it before serving to make sure it's cool enough.

If the food won't be eaten the next day, freeze it for later. Although we are not advocates of frozen food in general, freezing baby food, especially purées, is extremely practical and ensures that there is always good homemade food available. Your baby's consumption of those first solids will be very small, so you will always have more food than is required, unless you eat the rest yourself, which may be tempting. Place leftovers in a plastic ice cube tray, cover it tightly with aluminum foil, and freeze it. When frozen solid, remove the cubes and place them in a freezer bag for later use. Mark the date and contents on the bag.

Ice cube trays aren't the only choice for freezing. Less liquid food can be placed in scoops or blobs on a tray or dish, covered with foil, and frozen. As with the ice cubes, once frozen solid, the blobs can be sealed in a freezer bag, dated, and stored.

Although it depends on the type, almost all frozen foods will keep for at least 2 months. Either thaw the frozen food overnight in the refrigerator or slowly heat it in a pan on the stove, stirring just until it is warm. Always taste the food to make sure that it is completely thawed and not too hot. Microwaves can be used—according to the defrost mode instructions—but you must make sure that the food is thoroughly stirred to eliminate hot and cold spots.

Never refreeze thawed food or baby food made with frozen vegetables or other frozen foods. It is a health hazard.

# Necessary Equipment

Cooking in my restaurant, Patina, and cooking at home present two vastly different scenarios. At the restaurant, I have legions of prep cooks to assemble my *mise en place*—the ingredients—all nicely chopped, shredded, peeled, sliced, or whatever is required to be prepared to the point of cooking. At home, since neither my wife nor I have much time, we rely for prepping on some handy appliances and the usual *batterie du cuisine*, that is, kitchen equipment.

You probably already have most of the equipment necessary to prepare the recipes in this book, but the following items are indispensable.

## BLENDER

A blender will be your most useful appliance once you start your baby on solid food. It produces a finer purée than a food processor and can truly liquefy food. A blender accessory, the mini-blend bowl, is very useful for blending small amounts of food and grinding cheese, nuts, and porridge.

## STICK BLENDER

A luxury, but a handy one, is the stick blender. In the mixing beaker that it comes with, you can quickly purée, blend, or whisk small portions of food. You can also use it right in saucepans on the stove or in serving bowls and avoid having more dishes to wash.

## FOOD PROCESSOR

The food processor is the all-around most useful appliance you can own. It chops, slices, mixes, and purées everything from vegetables to meat to egg whites to bread. The pulse feature, which redistributes the food each time it is pressed, allows you to finely control the degree of processing. They come in a variety of sizes, from 3 to 4 cups, to up to 14. Get the largest one that suits your needs and your budget. You'll find that as you become familiar with its features, you'll be using it constantly. You'll want to make sure you have room for it on your counter and possibly under your cupboards.

## STAND MIXER

The stand mixer, with its variety of useful attachments, can mix bread dough, beat egg whites into snowy peaks, cream butter, and even grind meat, with little human interaction, since the head moves in a circular fashion from the edge to the center of the bowl, thoroughly mixing the contents. Especially popular with serious home bakers, stand mixers come in several capacities and horsepowers. Choose one based on your budget and requirements.

## HAND MIXER

Once the principle piece of equipment in most kitchens, the hand mixer has taken a back seat to its more capable successors, the food processor and the stand mixer. It still has its uses, however. Light, compact, and mobile, it can mix relatively small amounts at a choice of several speeds.

## STEAMERS

Steamers come in a variety of materials and styles from the simple, collapsible metal insert to the traditional Asian bamboo steamer to a three-tiered stainless steel model. Steaming not only retains nutrients but—in the two- and three-tiered steamers—allows for several components of a meal to be cooked at once. Christine's dad, a naturopathy enthusiast, is a firm believer in steaming.

## STRAINERS AND SIEVES

Both implements separate liquid from solids but do so to different degrees. Strainers usually have a coarser mesh or holes, such as a colander; sieves, with their finer mesh, are also used for dry ingredients, such as flour, confectioners' sugar, and powders. Sieves are available in a variety of sizes and materials. There is the large, flat-bottomed drum sieve, for large amounts; the cup-size flour sifter with a trigger handle; and the chinois, a conical sieve with a shaped-to-fit wooden pestle that extracts every last drop from cooked vegetables and other mixtures. Sieves can be used to smooth out gravies and remove seeds from raspberries. Until your baby is six months old, you'll be using a sieve constantly to make sure there are no fruit seeds or lumps in the purées.

## POTATO RICER

The potato ricer banishes lumps from mashed potatoes, other cooked root vegetables, and firm-fleshed fruit, such as apples. When pressed through the ricer, boiled potato emerges in soft rice-size bits. The ricer can be found in either metal or plastic models and some have interchangeable screens with a range of hole sizes.

## WOODEN SPOONS

The most obvious advantage of a wooden spoon is that it doesn't conduct heat. It feels good in the hand and is the preferred utensil for stirring risotto, making gravy, and deglazing a pan. Look for spoons made of boxwood or beech, which won't react with food and won't easily splinter or crack.

## DUTCH OVEN

A cast-iron round or oval pot with small handles on either side, the Dutch oven is the pot to use for braising and stews. It can go from the stovetop into the oven and, if attractively clad in enamel, can be placed on the table for serving. It has a flat, thick base for browning and evenly distributing heat, and can hold from 2 to 13 quarts.

## ICE CUBE TRAYS

Ice cube trays are perfect for freezing purées or soups in convenient sizes. Large, flexible plastic or rubber trays are best, making it easy to remove individual cubes.

## PARCHMENT PAPER

Impervious to grease and moisture, parchment paper is used to line baking pans.

# 1 tastes

## six to nine months

With our boys, we made the transition from breast-feeding to "solids" when they were four to five months old. That may feel too soon for many parents, which is why we have started the recipes at six months. By then vegetable and grain purées are usually being introduced into the baby's diet.

Between four and six months, your baby's digestive system will be developed enough to handle solid foods. Indications that your baby is ready are that she has doubled her birth weight and weighs at least thirteen to fifteen pounds; she's able to sit up with support and hold her head up; time between feedings decreases or she refuses the breast; and she stops thrusting her tongue out when you attempt to put a spoon in her mouth. Your baby may also begin to show interest in others eating and may attempt to feed herself. Your pediatrician, however, is the final authority on when to start your baby on solid food.

# roasted acorn squash purée

Squash is rich in beta-carotene, folic acid, and fiber, making it a good choice for your baby's diet. The brown sugar and cinnamon are optional, although they add a wonderful flavor to the squash and will make it enticing for older children and adults.

The squash can be prepared to the point before the chicken broth is added and kept in the refrigerator for up to 2 days. To finish, purée with the warmed chicken broth. Leftover purée can be frozen or mixed into yogurt or a soup.

**Makes 3 cups**

2 acorn squash, about 5 inches in diameter, halved and seeds and strings removed

3 tablespoons extra virgin olive oil

1/4 cup firmly packed dark brown sugar (optional)

1/4 teaspoon ground cinnamon (optional)

2 tablespoons low-sodium chicken broth, warmed

1. Preheat the oven to 400°F.

2. Set the squash halves cut side up, brush them with the oil, and sprinkle with the brown sugar and cinnamon. Wrap the halves in aluminum foil, place on a baking sheet, and roast for 30 to 40 minutes, until tender and easily pierced with the tip of a knife. Remove from the oven and set aside until cool enough to handle.

3. Scrape the flesh of the squash from the peel and transfer to a blender or food processor fitted with a steel blade. Add the warmed chicken broth and purée.

4. Serve immediately. Freeze leftover purée that won't be eaten the next day (see page 11).

# carrot with chicken broth purée

By eight to nine months, babies are ready for foods with a thicker texture than purées. At that point, depending on your baby's ability to chew, you can mash the carrot pieces instead of purée-ing them.

**Makes 2 cups**

2 cups low-sodium chicken broth

1 pound carrots, peeled and cut into 1/4-inch rounds

2 teaspoons unsalted butter, at room temperature

1. In a medium saucepan over high heat, bring the broth to a boil.

2. Add the carrots and cook for 10 to 12 minutes, until the carrots are tender and easily pierced with the tip of a knife. Remove the pan from the heat. Remove the carrots from the broth with a slotted spoon, reserving the liquid.

3. Combine the carrots and butter in a blender and purée, adding the reserved broth until the mixture is creamy.

4. Serve warm. Freeze leftover purée that won't be eaten the next day (see page 11).

# pea with mint purée

Peas were an early favorite with our kids because of their naturally sweet flavor. They also liked to throw them.

**Makes 1 cup**

2 cups freshly shelled peas

1 carrot, peeled and diced

1 celery stalk, trimmed and cut into small pieces

1 tablespoon unsalted butter, at room temperature

1/8 teaspoon minced fresh mint (optional)

1. Bring a large saucepan of water to a boil. Add the peas, carrot, and celery and cook for about 2 minutes, until the peas are bright green and tender. Remove from the heat and drain, reserving some liquid for puréeing. Refresh the vegetables in ice water and drain.

2. In a blender or food processor fitted with a steel blade, combine the vegetables with the butter and mint, and pulse until smooth, adding the reserved liquid as necessary to achieve the desired consistency.

3. Serve immediately. Freeze leftover purée that won't be eaten the next day (see page 11).

# couscous with corn and pea purée

We treat couscous as if it were a grain, when in fact it is tiny pasta. If time is critical, frozen peas and corn kernels can be used in this dish. The flavor and nutritional value, however, are always better with fresh.

**Makes 3 cups**

1 cup corn kernels, freshly
    scraped from the cob

1 cup freshly shelled peas

2 cups water

1 1/3 cups couscous

2 tablespoons unsalted butter

1. Bring a medium saucepan halfway filled with water to a boil. Add the corn and boil for about 2 minutes, until the corn is tender. Remove the kernels with a slotted spoon and set aside.

2. Add the peas to the same boiling water and boil for 2 minutes, until the peas are bright green and tender. Drain and refresh the peas in ice water. When cool, drain and set aside.

3. In a large saucepan, bring the 2 cups water to a boil. Add the couscous and the butter, stir, and cover. Decrease the heat to a simmer and cook for about 2 minutes.

4. Add the corn and peas to the couscous, remove from the heat, and let stand for about 5 minutes. Transfer to a blender or food processor fitted with a steel blade and pulse until smooth.

5. Serve immediately. Freeze leftover purée that won't be eaten the next day (see page 11). (If you have used frozen vegetables to make this, don't freeze the leftovers. Frozen food should never be refrozen after it has been thawed.)

# green beans and wax beans

At about seven months, your baby will be ready for green and wax beans. For older babies and uncivilized adults, green beans make great finger food. Mash or purée the beans until your baby is nine months old.

**Makes 3 cups**

3/4 pound green beans, trimmed

3/4 pound wax beans, trimmed

3 tablespoons unsalted butter

1/4 teaspoon minced garlic

1. In a large saucepan, bring a generous amount of water to a boil. Add the green beans to the boiling water and cook for 2 to 8 minutes, until bright green and tender, depending on the freshness of the beans. Remove the beans with a slotted spoon and refresh in ice water. Drain.

2. Bring the water back to a boil. Add the wax beans and cook for 2 to 8 minutes, depending on the freshness of the beans. Drain. Refresh the beans in ice water, then drain.

3. Heat the butter in a large sauté pan over medium-high heat. Add the garlic and cook for 2 minutes. Add the beans and sauté for about 3 minutes until warm, stirring to coat them evenly with the butter and garlic.

4. Serve immediately, if you are serving the beans whole. To purée, roughly chop and combine the beans in a blender with as much water as necessary to reach the desired consistency, about 1 cup. Freeze leftovers that won't be eaten the next day (see page 11).

# lentil with carrot purée

Brown lentils cook a little quicker than the smaller green French or Le Puy lentils, which have a better flavor, and which we prefer. We served this dish to our kids once or twice a week. Onions can be substituted for shallots. Omit the onions for babies younger than nine months.

**Makes about 3 cups**

4 cups low-sodium chicken broth

2 cups lentils, rinsed and picked over

2 carrots, peeled and finely chopped

1 teaspoon minced shallot or onion (optional)

1. In a large saucepan, combine the broth and lentils and bring to a boil. Add the carrots and shallot. Decrease the heat to a simmer and cook for about 30 minutes, until the lentils and vegetables are tender. Drain and reserve the liquid.

2. Transfer the lentil mixture to a blender and pulse until smooth, slowly adding the reserved cooking liquid.

3. Serve immediately. Freeze leftover purée that won't be eaten the next day (see page 11).

# pink lentil and peach purée

We like lentils and we like peaches. The two complement each other on the palate and, for an adult version, visually. This makes a good savory-sweet side dish. Double the ingredients to make four adult servings, and don't purée, of course. Pink lentils are sometimes referred to as red. Either can be used.

**Makes 1 cup**

2 fresh peaches, peeled, halved, and pitted

1/4 cup minced onion

3 tablespoons unsalted butter

2 1/2 cups low-sodium chicken broth, plus extra for purée, warmed

1/2 cup pink lentils, rinsed and picked over

1 teaspoon red wine vinegar

1. Preheat the oven to 350°F. Line a baking sheet with parchment paper.

2. Place the peach halves cut side up on the baking sheet and bake for about 30 minutes, until tender. When cool, cut the peaches into 1/2-inch dice.

3. In a medium saucepan, sauté the onion in the butter for about 3 minutes, until it softens. Add the 2 1/2 cups broth and bring to a boil over medium-high heat. Add the lentils and vinegar, and cook for 10 to 15 minutes, until most of the liquid has been absorbed. Add the peaches and cook for 1 to 2 minutes more.

4. Combine the lentil mixture in a blender or food processor fitted with a steel blade with about 1/4 cup warm broth and purée.

5. Serve warm or at room temperature. Freeze leftover purée that won't be eaten the next day (see page 11).

# rosemary bread sticks

Give these bread sticks an authentic Italian touch by flavoring them with rosemary leaves preserved in salt. This is easily prepared by sealing 1/4 cup rosemary leaves with an equal amount of sea salt in a jar with a lid. Let it sit for three days before use.

Salt can be reduced or eliminated from the recipe for children younger than two years old.

**Makes 28 bread sticks**

STARTER

1 package (2 1/2 teaspoons) active dry yeast

1 1/2 cups warm water

1/2 teaspoon sea salt (optional)

2 cups plus 1 tablespoon all-purpose flour

BREAD STICK DOUGH

1/4 cup extra virgin olive oil

1/4 cup fresh rosemary leaves, finely chopped

Sea salt and freshly ground black pepper (optional)

2 1/2 cups all-purpose flour

1. To make the starter, in the bowl of a stand mixer, dissolve the yeast in the water, and let it sit for 10 minutes. Add the salt and the 2 cups flour. Using the hook attachment, mix at low speed, gradually increasing to high until smooth.

2. Transfer the starter to a bowl and sprinkle with the 1 tablespoon flour. Cover the bowl with plastic wrap or a damp dishtowel and set it in a warm, draft-free spot for about 1 hour, until the starter has doubled in size. (The starter has doubled in size when the tablespoon of flour is no longer visible or large cracks appear on top.)

3. To make the dough, transfer the starter to the bowl of the stand mixer with the hook attachment. Add the oil, rosemary, salt, and pepper, and mix well on low. With the mixer on low speed, add the flour in 1/2-cup increments. Repeat until 2 cups of flour have been added and the dough forms into a sticky ball.

4. Preheat the oven to 400°F. Grease a sheet pan very lightly with olive oil.

5. Turn the dough out onto a lightly floured surface. Sprinkle it with the remaining 1/2 cup of flour, and knead by hand for about 10 minutes, until the dough is smooth and elastic.

6. Take a 1-ounce portion of dough and roll it on the work surface with both hands in a back-and-forth motion, moving your hands outward as the stick takes shape. Sprinkle it with flour only if the dough sticks to the work surface. Roll out to 16 to 18 inches in length and 1/4 inch in diameter. The sticks needn't be identical; the charm is their hand-rolled appearance.

7. Lay the sticks on the baking sheet. Bake for 5 to 8 minutes, until crisp and brown. Remove the bread sticks from the oven and let cool.

8. Serve as a snack or with a meal.

# 2 nibbles
## nine to twelve months

Around nine months, we began adding meat, poultry, and fish to the boys' meals. In fact, we often just minced up a little of what we were eating. The texture of the food can be chunkier as babies learn to chew. Many of the purées from the previous chapter can be simply mashed for babies in this age group.

Serving sizes, other than for purées, are for two adults and two to four children, depending on the ages of the children and whether the dish will be served as a main course or side dish for adults.

# broccoli and cauliflower purée

Since both these vegetables are excellent sources of vitamin C and other nutrients, you should try to make them a staple of your baby's diet before he or she develops any ideas on the subject.

**Makes 2 cups**

1/2 pound broccoli florets, cut into 3-inch pieces

1/2 pound cauliflower florets, cut into 3-inch pieces, core trimmed away

1/4 cup unsalted butter

1/2 cup low-sodium chicken broth, plus extra for puréeing, warmed

1. In a medium saucepan with a steamer, bring 2 inches of water to a boil.

2. Add the broccoli to the steamer, cover, and steam for 3 to 5 minutes, until the broccoli is bright green and tender. When done, refresh the broccoli in ice water. Remove the broccoli and drain.

3. Repeat the steaming procedure with fresh water for the cauliflower. Steam for 5 to 7 minutes, until the cauliflower is tender. Remove the cauliflower from the steamer and set aside. Don't refresh it in ice water.

4. Melt the butter in a sauté pan and sauté the broccoli and cauliflower for 1 minute.

5. Combine the broccoli and cauliflower in a blender or food processor fitted with a steel blade and pulse until smooth. Add the 1/2 cup broth to the mixture and pulse again until smooth. You may need to add a little more broth, depending upon the consistency of the purée.

6. Serve warm or at room temperature. Freeze leftover purée that won't be eaten the next day (see page 11).

# celery root purée

Celery root—or celeriac, as it is also known—is commonly prepared for babies and children in Europe. It makes good comfort food with a flavor a bit more intense than celery.

**Makes 1 1/4 cups**

1 pound celery root, peeled and cut into small cubes

2 tablespoons unsalted butter, at room temperature

10 to 15 leaves (1 ounce) fresh basil, thinly sliced, for garnish (optional)

1. Bring a large saucepan of water to a boil. Add the celery root and cook for about 10 minutes, until tender. Drain the celery root, reserving the liquid for puréeing.

2. Transfer the celery root to a blender or food processor fitted with a steel blade and purée. Add the butter and pulse until blended, adding the reserved liquid if necessary to achieve the desired consistency.

3. Serve immediately. For babies one year and older sprinkle the purée with the basil. Freeze leftover purée that won't be eaten the next day (see page 11).

# carrot purée with lemon

Their bright color and slightly sweet flavor make carrots popular with babies. The fact that they are also a major source of beta-carotene, which the body converts into vitamin A, makes them popular with parents.

Stir in 1$^1$/2 cups of warmed chicken stock to transform the purée into a delicious soup for two adults.

**Makes 2$^1$/2 cups**

1 pound carrots, peeled and chopped into 1-inch pieces

3/4 cup whole milk

3 tablespoons unsalted butter, melted

1 teaspoon freshly squeezed lemon juice

Minced fresh parsley, for garnish (optional)

1. Bring a medium saucepan filled with water to a boil. Add the carrots and cook for 10 minutes, until the carrots are tender and easily pierced with a knife. Remove the carrots with a slotted spoon and set aside.

2. In a small saucepan, combine the milk and butter and heat until the butter is melted.

3. Transfer the milk mixture to a blender with the carrots and purée until smooth. Stir in the lemon juice.

4. Garnish with the parsley and serve warm or at room temperature. Freeze leftover purée that won't be eaten the next day (see page 11).

# parsnips, apples, and sweet onions

Parsnips are sweet and delicious and very popular in Europe. They are best in the fall; pick small firm ones, about five to a pound. Larger ones will need to be cored. Maui onions, which are also sweet, are a good choice for this dish. This makes a great side dish for adults.

**Serves 4**

1 1/2 pounds parsnips, peeled and cut into large dice

2 tablespoons unsalted butter

1 tablespoon diced sweet onion

1 1/2 tablespoons sugar

3 apples, such as Braeburn or Fuji, peeled, cored, and cut into bite-size pieces

1. In a medium saucepan with a steamer, bring 2 inches of water to a boil.

2. Add the parsnips to the steamer, cover, and steam for 10 minutes, until the parsnips are tender and easily pierced with a knife. Remove the parsnips from the steamer and drain.

3. In a large sauté pan over medium heat, melt the butter. Add the parsnips and onion, sprinkle them with the sugar, and cook, stirring frequently, for 5 to 8 minutes, until the parsnips are glazed and dark brown but not burned. This will reduce the bitter aftertaste of the parsnips.

4. Add the apples and cook for about 5 minutes, until tender.

5. Mash well for babies nine to twelve months old. Serve immediately.

# potato and leek purée

An infant version of vichyssoise, this is for the nine-month-old—and older—baby with a discriminating palate. It can be served warm or at room temperature.

**Makes 1¹/2 cups**

1 pound Yukon gold potatoes, peeled, washed, and quartered

2 leeks, trimmed, cleaned, and cut into 1-inch pieces

2 tablespoons unsalted butter

¹/2 cup whole milk

1. In a large pot with water just to cover, boil the potatoes and leeks for about 30 minutes, until the potatoes are tender and easily pierced with the tip of a knife. Drain, reserving the water, and remove the potatoes. Pass them through a ricer. Set aside.

2. Transfer the leeks to a food processor fitted with a steel blade and purée.

3. Melt the butter in a heavy saucepan over medium heat. Add the riced potatoes. Gradually stir in the milk, beating with a wooden spoon until creamy. Stir in the puréed leeks. Stir in some of the reserved potato water if a more liquid consistency is desired.

4. Serve immediately. Freeze leftover purée that won't be eaten the next day (see page 11).

# creamed spinach

If there are any adults around when this is served, your baby will be lucky to get a nibble. Season with sea salt and freshly ground pepper for children over two years old and adults.

**Makes 2 cups**

1 pound fresh spinach, washed and stemmed

1 shallot, minced, or
   1 tablespoon minced onion

¼ cup unsalted butter

1 tablespoon all-purpose flour

1 cup heavy cream

¼ cup low-sodium chicken broth, for puréeing

1. Heat a large sauté pan over medium-high heat. Add the spinach with just the water that clings to its leaves. Add the shallot and cook, turning the spinach frequently with tongs, for about 3 minutes, until bright green. Remove the spinach and shallot from the pan and let cool. Finely chop and set aside.

2. In the same pan over medium-high heat, melt the butter and add the flour. Cook for 2 minutes, stirring constantly with a whisk. Decrease the heat to medium, add the cream, and whisk until smooth. Cook for 1 to 2 minutes. Add the spinach, stirring frequently with a wooden spoon until well blended.

3. For babies nine to twelve months, purée the mixture in a blender, adding the broth until the mixture is smooth. For older babies and adults, don't purée.

4. Serve warm. Freeze leftovers that won't be eaten the next day (see page 11).

# sweet peas and ham

The salty flavor of the ham makes a good contrast with the sweetness of the peas. Seek out nitrate-free ham, which is now widely available.

**Serves 4**

3 cups freshly shelled peas

1/4 cup low-sodium chicken broth, plus extra warm broth for puréeing

4 ounces good-quality, low-sodium, nitrate-free ham, cut into 1/4-inch dice

1 tablespoon unsalted butter

1. Bring a medium saucepan filled with water to a boil over high heat. Add the peas and cook for about 3 minutes, until bright green and tender. Drain and refresh in ice water. When cool, drain the peas, and set aside.

2. Heat the 1/4 cup broth to a boil in a small saucepan, decrease to a simmer, and add the ham. Cook for 1 minute, and then add the cooked peas, stirring for about 2 minutes, until warm. Stir in the butter.

3. Serve immediately. For babies nine to twelve months old, purée the peas and ham in a blender with the extra warmed chicken broth. Add more broth, if necessary, to achieve the desired consistency. Freeze leftovers that won't be eaten the next day (see page 11).

# black beans and banana

I first encountered black beans in Miami. The sweet banana, with slightly tart crème fraîche for babies older than one year, offers a nice contrast to the beans. Crème fraîche, which is tangier than plain cream and less sour than sour cream, can be purchased in most grocery stores.

**Serves 4**

2 tablespoons extra virgin olive oil

1/2 medium onion, minced

1 1/2 cups black beans, rinsed and picked over

8 cups low-sodium chicken broth

Leaves of 2 sprigs fresh thyme

2 ripe bananas, cubed

Crème fraîche, for garnish (optional)

1. Heat the oil in a large, heavy-bottomed pan over medium-high heat for 1 minute. Add the onion and sauté for about 3 minutes, until translucent.

2. Add the beans, broth, and thyme leaves, and bring to a boil. Decrease the heat to medium, cover, and cook for 1 1/2 hours, until the beans are tender and most of the liquid has been absorbed. Check occasionally to skim any foam from the surface, if necessary.

3. To serve, place a serving of beans into a bowl and top with the banana pieces. Mash for babies younger than one year. Garnish with 1 teaspoon crème fraîche for babies older than one year and adults.

# couscous with cauliflower and carrots

Despite being rich in vitamins and fiber, this is a dish our boys actually like quite a bit. Sea salt is included as an option for children over two years old and adults.

**Serves 4**

4 carrots, peeled and finely chopped

1 cup finely chopped cauliflower florets

1 1/3 cups low-sodium chicken broth

1 1/2 tablespoons unsalted butter

1 cup couscous

Sea salt (optional)

1. In a medium saucepan with a steamer, bring 2 inches of water to a boil.

2. Add the carrots and cauliflower and steam for 10 to 12 minutes, until the vegetables are tender. Drain and set aside.

3. In a small pan, heat the broth over medium-high heat.

4. Melt the butter in a medium saucepan over medium-high heat. Stir in the couscous, stirring to coat well with the butter, and cook for 1 minute. Add the broth, cover, and cook over low heat for about 4 minutes, until the broth is absorbed. Stir in the carrots and cauliflower. Season with salt.

5. Serve slightly warm or at room temperature. Freeze leftovers than won't be eaten the next day (see page 11).

# turnips, pears, and parsley

Ripe pears and a little sugar caramelize and transform the simple turnip. Make sure the pears are very ripe. For adults, this makes a great side dish for chicken, duck, or quail.

**Serves 4**

1½ pounds turnips, peeled and
    cut into cubes

2 tablespoons unsalted butter

¼ cup sugar

2 ripe Bartlett pears, peeled,
    cored, and quartered

Minced fresh parsley, for
    garnish (optional)

1. Bring a large saucepan half filled with water to a boil. Add the turnips and decrease the heat to medium-high. Cook for 10 to 12 minutes, until the turnips are tender but firm. Remove the turnips from the water and set aside to drain.

2. Melt the butter in a sauté pan over medium-high heat. Add the turnips; sprinkle them with the sugar, and cook, turning frequently, for about 5 minutes, until they are tender and caramelized. Add the pears and sauté for about 2 minutes more.

3. Mash for babies nine to eighteen months old. Garnish with parsley and serve immediately.

# sweet potato risotto

Arborio rice, which is grown in the north of Italy, is the rice traditionally used to make authentic risotto. The fat, starchy grains give the dish its characteristic creamy texture. Other short-grain rice can be substituted, but the results will not be as satisfying. When preparing this for an older audience, you can substitute Parmesan cheese for a more mature flavor.

**Serves 4 to 6**

4 large sweet potatoes

5¹/₂ cups low-sodium chicken broth

4 tablespoons unsalted butter

¹/₂ cup minced onion

1¹/₂ cups Arborio rice

¹/₂ cup grated Cheddar cheese

Leaves of 1 sprig fresh thyme

1. Preheat the oven to 375°F.

2. Wash the sweet potatoes, pierce each several times with the tip of a knife, and bake for 1 to 1 1/2 hours, until tender. Remove them from the oven and let cool. Peel the sweet potatoes and transfer the flesh to a food processor fitted with a steel blade. Purée until smooth.

3. Heat the broth in a saucepan over low heat.

4. In a large pan, melt 1 tablespoon of the butter over medium-high heat. Add the onion and sauté for about 3 minutes, until translucent. Decrease the heat to low. Add the rice and, using a wooden spoon, stir for 2 minutes, until all the grains are well coated. Stir in the broth, 1/2 cup at a time. When each addition of broth is almost completely absorbed, add the next 1/2 cup, stirring frequently. Continue adding the broth until it has all been added and absorbed and the rice is tender but firm.

5. Stir in the puréed sweet potatoes, the cheese, the remaining 3 tablespoons of butter, and the thyme leaves. Stir until creamy. Serve warm. Freeze leftovers that won't be eaten the next day (see page 11).

# banana peach compote

Bananas are rich in potassium and fiber and one of the easiest foods to prepare for your baby. This is best, of course, with fresh, ripe peaches.

Purée for babies, depending on their ability to chew. For adults, serve this over granola for breakfast or with pound cake for dessert.

**Makes 3¹/2 cups**

¹/2 cup water

6 tablespoons sugar

1 teaspoon freshly squeezed
    lemon juice

1 strip lemon zest (optional)

4 large fresh peaches, peeled,
    pitted, and quartered

2 ripe bananas, cut into 1-inch
    cubes

¹/2 cup plain yogurt

1. In a medium saucepan, combine the water and sugar and bring to a simmer, swirling the pan once or twice. When the sugar has dissolved, add the lemon juice and zest.

2. Decrease the heat until the syrup is barely simmering; add the peaches and cook, uncovered, for about 15 minutes, until the peaches are tender. Remove the pan from the heat and let the peaches cool in the liquid for 30 minutes. Remove the cooled peaches with a slotted spoon, chop into small pieces, and place in a bowl.

3. With a wooden spoon, carefully fold the bananas and yogurt into the peaches until blended. Serve immediately. Freeze leftovers that won't be eaten the next day (see page 11).

# 3 bites

## one to two years

By the time they were a year old our boys were eating almost exactly what we were eating, with a few modifications. This is also when their particular food fetishes began to develop.

Serving sizes, other than for purées, are for two adults and two to four children, depending on the ages of the children and whether the dish will be served as a main course or side dish for adults.

# lentils with apple-smoked bacon

Many of the dishes of my childhood were flavored with bacon, and I naturally used it in the dishes I prepared for my boys after they were a year old. It's now possible to buy nitrate-free bacon, which makes using it more attractive.

**Serves 4**

1/4 pound apple-smoked bacon, finely chopped

1 medium onion, minced

2 carrots, peeled and diced

1 celery stalk, trimmed and thinly sliced

1 1/2 cups low-sodium chicken broth

2 cups water

1/2 cup brown lentils, rinsed and picked over

1/2 cup green lentils, rinsed and picked over

1/2 cup pink lentils, rinsed and picked over

Leaves from 1 sprig fresh thyme

1. In a large, heavy pot over medium heat, cook the bacon for about 4 minutes, until the fat is translucent. Add the onion and sauté for about 3 minutes, until it is soft. Stirring with a wooden spoon, add the carrots and celery and cook for 2 minutes.

2. Add the broth, water, lentils, and thyme leaves. Cover, decrease the heat to medium, and cook for about 30 minutes, until the lentils are tender and most of the liquid is absorbed.

3. Serve immediately. Freeze leftovers that won't be eaten the next day (see page 11).

# brown rice with hazelnut and apple purée

This was one of our boys' favorite dishes, and it's a good way to safely introduce nuts—which are full of essential fatty acids, B vitamins, and vitamin E—into their diet.

Before you purée it for your baby, put a little in a bowl with a few hazelnut pieces and raisins for your own breakfast. If there is a family history of allergies to nuts, wait until your child is three to introduce them.

**Makes 2 cups**

1/4 cup hazelnuts (optional)

2 cups water

1 cup brown rice

2 Braeburn or Rome apples, peeled, cored, and cut into 1-inch pieces

1 tablespoon sugar

1/2 cup apple juice

1. Place the hazelnuts on a baking sheet and toast for about 10 minutes, until lightly browned. Remove and let cool.

2. In a large saucepan, bring the 2 cups water to a boil. Add the rice, cover, and reduce the heat to a simmer. Cook for about 40 minutes, until the rice is tender and the water is absorbed. Remove from the heat.

3. In a medium saucepan, combine the apples with water just to cover. Add the sugar and cook over high heat for about 8 minutes, until the apples are tender. Drain.

4. While the apples are cooking, finely grind the toasted hazelnuts in a mini blender or a food processor fitted with a steel blade.

5. Fold the apples into the cooked rice. Transfer the rice-apple mixture into a food processor fitted with a steel blade and pulse, gradually adding the apple juice, until smooth. Transfer the mixture to a bowl and fold in the hazelnuts.

6. Serve immediately. Freeze leftover purée that won't be eaten the next day (see page 11).

# grits and spinach with cheddar

Years ago I did a consulting job in Georgia, where I was introduced to grits with gravy. Grits are very similar to polenta, and the texture is great for babies. Good-quality grits, which are white and coarsely ground, can be found at high-end grocery stores, health food stores, and online. Recommended Cheddars are Bravo from California and Herkimer from upstate New York, but any good-quality Cheddar will work well.

**Serves 4**

8 ounces fresh spinach,
 washed and stemmed

3 cups water

3/4 cup good-quality grits

1 tablespoon unsalted butter

3/4 cup grated good-quality
 Cheddar

1. In a sauté pan over medium heat, cook the spinach with just the water that clings to its leaves for 2 to 3 minutes, until the spinach is wilted and bright green. Remove the spinach and refresh in ice water. When the spinach is cool, drain it and squeeze out the excess moisture. Very finely chop it and set aside.

2. In a medium saucepan, combine the water and grits and bring to a boil over medium-high heat. Decrease the heat to a simmer and stir with a wire whisk to eliminate any lumps. Cover and cook, stirring occasionally with a wooden spoon, for 5 to 10 minutes for quick-cooking grits, 15 to 20 minutes for regular grits, until all the water is absorbed.

3. Decrease the heat to low and stir in the butter. Add the cheese, stirring until it is melted. Stir in the spinach.

4. Serve immediately. Freeze leftovers that won't be eaten the next day (see page 11).

# chicken pot pie

This is a great one-dish lunch or dinner for the entire family. Phyllo dough can be used for convenience, or use your favorite pie crust recipe. Mash the filling with a little of the crust for babies who aren't ready for lumpy food.

**Serves 6**

2 pounds boneless, skinless chicken breasts or thighs

3/4 cup freshly shelled peas

5 1/2 tablespoons unsalted butter, plus 1 tablespoon melted

15 pearl onions, peeled

3 medium carrots, peeled and cut into 1/4-inch pieces

2 small celery stalks, trimmed and cut into 1/4-inch pieces

1/2 cup all-purpose flour

1 1/2 cups whole milk

Sea salt and freshly ground black pepper (optional)

1/2 teaspoon fresh thyme leaves

1 (16-ounce) package phyllo dough (defrosted as per instructions on box)

1. Bring a medium saucepan of lightly salted water to a boil. Meanwhile, cut the chicken into 1-inch cubes. Add the chicken and cook, uncovered, for about 5 minutes, until tender. Drain the meat and transfer it to a large bowl. Reserve the broth and set aside.

2. Bring a medium saucepan of lightly salted water to a boil. Add the peas and cook for about 2 to 3 minutes, until the peas are bright green and tender. Drain and refresh in ice water. When cool, drain the peas and set aside.

3. Melt 1 1/2 tablespoons of the butter in a sauté pan over medium-high heat. Add the onions, carrots, and celery, and sauté for about 5 minutes. Add 1/4 cup of the reserved chicken broth, and cook for 5 more minutes. Drain the vegetables and set aside.

4. Melt 4 tablespoons of the butter in a heavy-bottomed saucepan over medium heat. Stir in the flour and cook for about 3 minutes, until the mixture browns. Decrease the heat to a simmer and slowly add 2 cups of the reserved broth, whisking until smooth. Whisk in the milk and simmer, continuing to whisk until the sauce thickens. Season with salt and pepper.

continued

5. Fold the chicken, sautéed vegetables, and peas into the sauce with a wooden spoon and mix well. Stir in the thyme. (The dish can be made to this point one day in advance. Remove the mixture from the refrigerator and let it reach room temperature before topping it with the pastry.)

6. Pour the mixture into six individual 5-inch ovenproof baking dishes or one 9 by 11 by 1 3/4-inch baking dish.

7. Preheat the oven to 400°F. Unroll six or seven sheets of phyllo dough for each dish. Cut the dough to fit the inside dimensions of the dish.

8. Fill the baking dish (or dishes) with the chicken mixture and lay one sheet of phyllo dough on top. Brush lightly with the remaining 1 tablespoon melted butter. To prevent the edges from cracking, lightly brush the edges first and work in toward the center. Repeat for each layer, including the top layer. The pie, or pies, can be frozen at this point and baked later.

9. Bake individual pies for about 15 minutes, one large pie for 20 to 30 minutes, until the pastry is golden brown and the filling is bubbling.

10. Let cool slightly and serve. The large or individual pies can be frozen before being baked. To bake, the pie or pies should be removed from the refrigerator 1 hour before.

# white fish in mashed potatoes

Any white, flaky fish fresh from the market can be used for this dish. This is a simple version of brandade, a French Provençal dish served as either a main course or a side dish. Sea salt and pepper are included in the recipe for children over two years old and adults.

**Serves 4**

MASHED POTATOES

1 pound Yukon gold potatoes, peeled and quartered

1/2 cup whole milk

1/4 cup unsalted butter

1 1/4 cups yogurt

Sea salt and freshly ground black pepper (optional)

WHITE FISH

1 1/2 pounds white fish fillets, such as ling cod or halibut

Sea salt and freshly ground black pepper (optional)

1/4 cup extra virgin olive oil

Juice of 1/2 lemon

1 tablespoon thinly sliced fresh basil, for garnish (optional)

1. To prepare the potatoes, bring a large pot of lightly salted water to a boil. Add the potatoes and boil for 20 to 30 minutes, until the potatoes are tender and easily pierced with a knife. Drain the potatoes and set aside to cool. When cool enough to handle, press the potatoes through a ricer.

2. Preheat the oven to 250°F.

3. In the same large pot, heat the milk and butter. Return the potatoes to the pot and stir until smooth. Add the yogurt and continue to stir. Season with salt and pepper. Cover the potatoes with aluminum foil and place in the oven to keep warm.

4. To prepare the fish, season the fillets with salt and pepper, and in a large sauté pan combine 1/2 inch water with the oil and lemon juice and bring to a boil. Decrease the heat to medium and cook for 1 minute. Place the fillets in the water and cover. Decrease the heat to a simmer and poach the fish for about 5 minutes, until flaky.

5. To serve, for children one to three years old flake a portion of the fish and blend it into the mashed potatoes. For adults, place a portion of mashed potatoes on individual plates and position a piece of fish on top. Pour the reserved natural juices from the pan over the fish and for adults garnish with the basil.

# cheddar cheese muffins

My boys love it when I can persuade my wife to make these. Warm, cheesy muffins are a great way to start the day, and they're rich in protein and calcium. We've found that we get the best results with Arrowhead cornmeal. The salt can be left out for children under two years old.

**Makes 18 regular or 36 mini muffins**

10 green onions, roots and ends trimmed

Olive oil for coating onions

1/2 teaspoon sea salt, plus more for seasoning (optional)

1 cup whole milk

1/2 cup buttermilk

1 large egg

1 3/4 cups all-purpose flour

1 cup yellow cornmeal

1/4 cup sugar

2 teaspoons baking powder

1/2 teaspoon baking soda

1/2 cup unsalted butter

1 1/2 cups shredded good-quality Cheddar cheese

1. Preheat the oven to 400°F. Rub a baking sheet with oil.

2. Lightly coat the onions with olive oil, place them on the baking sheet, and season with salt. Roast for 5 to 8 minutes, until lightly browned. Chop into small dice.

3. Decrease the oven to 375°F. Grease the muffin tins with butter.

4. In a small bowl, whisk together the milk, buttermilk, and egg. In a separate bowl, combine the flour, cornmeal, sugar, baking powder, baking soda, and 1/2 teaspoon salt.

5. In the bowl of a stand mixer fitted with the paddle, cream the butter on high speed until smooth. Switch to low speed, and add the flour mixture alternating with the milk mixture until smooth. Add the cheese and green onions. Mix just to blend.

6. Use a small ice-cream scoop, or measure 2 tablespoons of batter into each cup of the regular muffin tins or about 1 tablespoon of batter into the mini. Bake on the center rack of the oven for about 20 minutes for the regular size, 15 minutes for the mini, until the tops are golden and a toothpick inserted into the center comes out clean.

7. Let cool on a rack for 5 minutes before serving. Extra muffins can be refrigerated for up to 2 days or frozen for 2 weeks.

# banana purée with ground hazelnuts

Ground hazelnuts add nutrition and interest to simple puréed bananas. If there is a family history of allergies to nuts, wait until your child is three to introduce them.

**Makes 1¹/2 cups**

¹/4 cup hazelnuts (optional)

4 ripe bananas, puréed or mashed

1 tablespoon freshly squeezed lemon juice

1. Preheat the oven to 400°F.

2. Place the hazelnuts on a baking sheet and toast for about 10 minutes, until lightly browned. Let cool, then finely grind the nuts in a blender or a food processor fitted with a steel blade.

3. Add the bananas and pulse until well blended. Add the lemon juice and pulse a few more times to blend.

4. Serve immediately. Freeze leftovers that won't be eaten the next day (see page 11).

# rice pudding

Everyone's favorite, this pudding can be puréed if your baby is not able to manage lumps yet. Adults and older children will happily consume this with a little fruit compote—or without—for breakfast.

**Serves 4**

5 cups whole milk

3/4 cup sugar

4 cinnamon sticks

1 cup short-grain rice

1/2 teaspoon ground cinnamon

Pinch of ground nutmeg

1. In a heavy medium saucepan, combine the milk and sugar with the cinnamon sticks and bring to a boil, stirring constantly with a whisk for about 2 minutes, until the sugar is dissolved.

2. Decrease the heat to a simmer, add the rice, cover, and cook, stirring occasionally with a wooden spoon, for about 1 hour, until most of the milk has been absorbed and the texture is creamy.

3. Remove the cinnamon sticks and stir in the ground cinnamon and nutmeg.

4. Serve the pudding warm or refrigerate and serve chilled.

# crème caramel

Who, child or adult, doesn't love crème caramel? Traditional in Europe and in Mexico, where it is known as flan, crème caramel has always been a favorite treat for our boys. To make a richer version for older children and adults, substitute cream for the milk.

**Serves 6**

CARAMEL

1 cup sugar

¼ cup water

1 tablespoon lemon juice

CUSTARD

3 large eggs

3 egg yolks

¾ cup sugar

4 cups whole milk, heated

1 vanilla bean

1. To make the caramel, combine the sugar, water, and lemon juice in a small, nonaluminum saucepan and bring to a simmer. Without stirring, let the sugar dissolve into a clear liquid and cover the pan.

2. Boil the syrup for several minutes over medium-high heat, again without stirring, until the bubbles are thick. Uncover the pan and continue boiling, swirling the pan occasionally.

3. As the syrup begins to color, continue to swirl until it is an even golden brown. Remove the pan from the heat and continue swirling. Immediately pour the caramel into a baking dish; tip to coat the bottom and halfway up the sides of the pan.

4. Preheat the oven to 350°F.

5. To make the custard, blend the eggs, yolks, and sugar in a bowl with a whisk, being careful to avoid creating foam. Gradually blend in the heated milk to dissolve the sugar completely, stirring carefully to minimize foam. Split the vanilla bean lengthwise and scrape the seeds into the bowl. Add the bean to the mixture, cover, and let steep for 10 minutes. Discard the vanilla bean and pour the mixture through a strainer into the baking dish with the caramel. Skim off any bubbles.

continued

6. Set the baking dish in a larger pan, and fill the larger pan with hot water to halfway up the side of the baking dish. Set the pan in the oven and check occasionally to make sure the water remains at a simmer. Boiling water will make the custard grainy. After 45 to 50 minutes, check the center with a toothpick; it should come out clean but the custard will still wiggle a bit.

7. Let the custard cool to room temperature. To serve, run a thin knife between the custard and the baking dish, invert a serving plate on top of the baking dish, and turn it over. The custard will slip out and the caramel will pool around the bottom. Cut into wedges and spoon some of the caramel over each piece. Leftovers can be stored in the refrigerator for up to 2 days.

# peach honey compote

Make this only when you have fresh peaches at the peak of the season. Because this contains honey, it's not suitable for children younger than a year old.

**Serves 4**

1/4 cup water

2 tablespoons good-quality honey

1 teaspoon freshly squeezed lemon or lime juice

4 large or 6 medium ripe peaches, peeled, pitted, and finely chopped

1. In a medium saucepan, combine the water, honey, and lemon juice. Bring to a boil and boil for 1 minute.

2. Decrease the heat to a simmer and add the peaches. Cook for about 5 minutes, depending on the ripeness of the fruit, until the peaches are tender but not mushy. Let cool.

3. Serve at room temperature. Leftovers can be refrigerated for up to 2 days or frozen for up to 2 months (see page 11).

# plum honey compote

Any stone fruit in season can be used in this compote: cherries, peaches, or apricots. Remember, no honey for babies under a year.

**Serves 4**

1 cup water

1 teaspoon freshly squeezed lemon juice

1/2 cup honey

16 assorted plums, peeled, pitted, and cut into 1/2-inch pieces

1/4 cup golden raisins

Zest of 1 lemon

1 strip orange zest

1. In a large saucepan, combine the water, lemon juice, and honey and bring to a boil. Boil for 3 minutes.

2. Add the plums, raisins, lemon zest, and orange zest. Decrease the heat to a simmer. Cook for about 5 minutes, until the plums are tender but not mushy. Watch the plums closely; depending on their freshness, they can become too soft very quickly. Let cool.

3. Serve at room temperature. Leftovers can be refrigerated for up to 2 days or frozen for up to 2 months (see page 11).

# 4 meals

## two to three years

Although the recipes in this chapter don't constitute meals in themselves, we chose the title "Meals" because at this age our babies had grown into toddlers and were able to sit at the tables in high chairs and take part, very enthusiastically, in family meals.

Serving sizes, other than for purées, are for two adults and two to four children, depending on the ages of the children and whether the dish will be served as a main course or side dish for adults.

# artichokes with extra virgin olive oil

Artichokes are not typical baby fare, but we always sought to broaden our babies' palates, and they were fascinated by the artichoke as an object. Leftover artichoke hearts can be used in a salad.

**Serves 4**

4 large artichokes

2 tablespoons freshly squeezed lemon juice

3 tablespoons extra virgin olive oil

Sea salt and freshly ground black pepper

1. Peel off the tough outer leaves of the artichoke. Trim around the base of the artichoke and cut the top leaves close to the artichoke heart without removing any flesh. Remove the fuzzy center with your fingers and, with a spoon, lightly scrape the cavity of the heart. Rub the heart with lemon juice to prevent it from discoloring.

2. In a medium saucepan with a steamer, bring 2 inches of water to a boil. Add the artichoke hearts to the steamer, cover, and cook for 15 to 25 minutes, until tender and easily pierced with the tip of a knife. Remove the cooked artichoke hearts and let cool.

3. Cut the cooled artichoke hearts into bite-size pieces and toss with the oil. Season with salt and pepper and serve.

# avocado with onion

Living in Southern California inspired my interest in avocados; they're such an integral part of the cuisine. In addition to their wonderful taste and texture, they provide vitamins A and C and unsaturated fatty acids, which are important, I've been told, for brain development. This also makes a great dip for the rest of the family.

**Makes 2 cups**

2 large avocados, halved, peeled, and pitted

1/4 tablespoon minced onion

2 tablespoons freshly squeezed lemon juice

Sea salt

Minced cilantro leaves, for garnish (optional)

1. Mash the avocado with a fork in a mixing bowl until smooth. (Reserve one of the avocado pits to place in the mixture to keep the avocado from turning brown if you're not serving it right away.)

2. Mix in the minced onion, lemon juice, and sea salt.

3. To serve, remove the pit (if necessary) and garnish with the minced cilantro leaves.

# beet and orange juice purée

Fortunately, our boys always liked beets, maybe for the color and slightly sweet flavor. This is a good source of iron and vitamin C for babies nine months and older.

**Makes 2 cups**

4 medium red, yellow, or orange beets

1 tablespoon extra virgin olive oil

1/4 cup freshly squeezed orange juice

1 teaspoon orange zest strips (optional)

1. Preheat the oven to 350°F.

2. Wash the beets but do not dry them, and coat with the oil. Wrap them individually in aluminum foil and place on a baking sheet.

3. Roast the beets for 30 to 40 minutes, until tender and easily pierced with the tip of a knife. Set aside until cool enough to handle.

4. Remove the beets from the foil, peel, and cut into quarters. Place the beets into a food processor fitted with a steel blade and purée them with the orange juice.

5. Serve immediately, sprinkled with a couple strips of orange zest.

# brussels sprouts with sweet onion

It was always a challenge to get our kids to eat Brussels sprouts, but they are so nutritious that we've tried a number of ways to make them appealing. This was pretty successful.

For babies twelve to eighteen months, this can be mashed or puréed in a blender or food processor with enough water to reach the desired consistency.

**Serves 4**

1/2 pound Brussels sprouts, trimmed and quartered

1 tablespoon extra virgin olive oil

1 tablespoon minced sweet onion

1 1/2 cups low-sodium chicken broth

1/2 teaspoon nutmeg (optional)

Sea salt and freshly ground black pepper

1. Bring a large pot of lightly salted water to a boil. Add the Brussels sprouts and cook for 10 to 12 minutes, until bright green. Drain the Brussels sprouts and refresh in ice water. When cool, remove them and set aside to drain.

2. Heat the oil in a large sauté pan over medium-high heat for 1 minute. Add the onion and Brussels sprouts and sauté for about 5 minutes, until the onion softens. Add the broth and nutmeg. Season with salt and pepper. Stir for 3 to 4 minutes to heat through.

3. Serve immediately.

# cabbage with lemon

We often served our boys cabbage because it is so rich in vitamin C. Babies must be at least eighteen months old to eat cabbage because it can be difficult to digest.

**Serves 4**

1½ pounds savoy or napa cabbage, cored and cut into ½-inch slices on the diagonal

1 tablespoon extra virgin olive oil

1 cup low-sodium chicken broth

1 teaspoon freshly squeezed lemon juice

Sea salt and freshly ground black pepper (optional)

1. Bring a large pot of lightly salted water to a boil and add the cabbage. Cook for 10 to 12 minutes, until the cabbage is bright green and tender. Drain the cabbage and refresh in ice water. When cool, drain and set the cabbage aside.

2. Heat the oil in a large sauté pan over moderate heat. Add the cabbage and broth. Cook for 5 to 8 minutes, until the cabbage is tender. Stir in the lemon juice and season with salt and pepper.

3. Serve immediately.

# peas, onions, and apple-smoked bacon

The distinctive smoked flavor of the bacon and the sweetness of the onion make this simple pea dish enticing enough for adults. Any type of onion can be substituted for the Maui, but sweet ones work best.

For babies six to twelve months old, omit the onion and bacon, and purée about 1/2 cup of the peas in the blender with enough of the broth to achieve a smooth consistency.

**Serves 4**

4 cups freshly shelled peas

1/3 pound apple-smoked bacon, finely diced

1 cup low-sodium chicken broth

1 medium Maui onion, diced

Sea salt and freshly ground black pepper

1. Bring a large saucepan of lightly salted water to a boil. Add the peas and cook for about 3 minutes, until the peas are bright green and tender. Drain the peas and refresh in ice water. When cool, drain them and set aside.

2. Refill the saucepan with water (do not add salt) and bring to a boil. Blanch the diced bacon in the water for 1 minute. Remove it from the heat, drain, and set the bacon aside.

3. Bring the broth to a boil in a large saucepan. Decrease the heat to medium-high, add the onion and bacon, and cook for 3 minutes. Stir in the peas and cook for 2 to 3 minutes, until the peas are hot.

4. Season with salt and pepper and serve immediately.

# garbanzo bean casserole

This dish is a product of the time I spent in Provence, where garbanzo beans are a common ingredient in salads and stews and the wonderful cracker known as socca.

For babies one to two years old, purée the beans in a food processor fitted with a steel blade, adding enough water to achieve the desired consistency.

**Serves 4**

2 cups dried garbanzo beans, rinsed and picked over

1/4 cup plus 3 tablespoons extra virgin olive oil

1 tablespoon minced onion

1 tablespoon freshly squeezed lemon juice

Leaves of 1 sprig fresh thyme

Sea salt and freshly ground black pepper (optional)

1. Soak the beans overnight in a bowl filled with cold water. Drain and rinse.

2. In a large casserole, heat the 1/4 cup oil over medium heat. Add the onion and cook for 3 to 4 minutes, until tender. Add the beans, lemon juice, and thyme leaves. Season with salt and pepper. Add water to cover the beans by 2 inches. Bring to a boil, then decrease the heat to medium. Cover and cook, stirring occasionally, for about 2 hours, depending on the age of the beans, until most of the liquid is absorbed and the beans are tender.

3. When the beans are done, stir in the remaining 3 tablespoons oil. Adjust the seasoning if necessary. Serve immediately.

# white beans and parsley

Known as *haricot blanc* in France, white beans are a staple of traditional dishes like cassoulet. When cooking beans, keep in mind that cooking time is greatly affected by the age of the beans; younger beans can cook twice as fast as older ones.

For babies from one to two years old, purée the beans in a food processor fitted with a steel blade, adding more chicken stock to achieve the desired consistency.

**Serves 4**

2 cups white or pinto beans, rinsed and picked over

3 tablespoons extra virgin olive oil

1 tablespoon chopped onion

6 cloves garlic, minced

1/2 cup finely diced apple-smoked bacon

4 to 5 cups low-sodium chicken broth

3 tablespoons finely chopped parsley

Sea salt and freshly ground black pepper

1. Soak the beans overnight in a bowl filled with cold water. Rinse and drain.

2. In a large casserole, heat the oil over medium-high heat for 1 minute. Decrease the heat to medium; add the onion, garlic, and bacon, and sauté for 2 to 3 minutes, until the bacon fat is translucent.

3. Add the broth and beans and bring to a boil. Decrease the heat and simmer for 30 to 40 minutes, until the beans are tender.

4. Stir in the parsley and season with salt and pepper. Serve immediately.

# wild rice risotto

Although a true risotto is made with Arborio rice, I call this a risotto because the cooking method is the same. Wild rice, which is actually a grass, adds texture and a nutty flavor, which I like.

For babies seven to nine months old, purée the rice with enough chicken broth to reach the desired consistency.

**Serves 4**

3 tablespoons unsalted butter

1 carrot, peeled and cut into
    small pieces

1 celery stalk, trimmed and cut
    into small pieces

1 1/2 cups wild rice, rinsed

4 cups low-sodium chicken
    broth, warmed

Sea salt and freshly ground
    black pepper

1. In a medium saucepan, melt 1 tablespoon of the butter over medium-high heat. Add the carrot and celery and sauté for 5 minutes. Decrease the heat to medium, add the rice, and cook for 1 minute, stirring constantly.

2. Add 1 cup of the broth and cook, stirring occasionally, until most of the liquid has been absorbed. At that point add another 1/2 cup of the broth and repeat the process for 25 to 35 minutes, until all the liquid has been absorbed. Stir in the remaining 2 tablespoons of butter.

3. Season with salt and pepper. Serve immediately.

# tomato risotto

Italian children are raised on risotto. You can whip up a batch with just about anything in the refrigerator. We began serving risotto to our boys when they were two years old.

**Serves 4 to 6**

1 1/2 pounds Roma tomatoes

2 tablespoons extra virgin
    olive oil

1 tablespoon finely chopped
    sweet onion

2 cups Arborio rice

6 cups low-sodium chicken
    broth, warmed

1/2 cup freshly grated
    Parmesan cheese

2 tablespoons unsalted butter

Sea salt and freshly ground
    black pepper

1 tablespoon thinly sliced
    basil leaves, for garnish
    (optional)

1. Bring a large saucepan of water to a boil. Add the tomatoes and blanch for 1 minute, until the skins begin to split. Remove the tomatoes from the water and set aside to cool, then peel, seed, and chop into small pieces.

2. Heat the oil in a medium heavy-bottomed pot over medium heat for 1 minute. Add the onion and sauté for 3 to 4 minutes, until translucent and tender. Add the rice and stir to coat with the oil for 1 to 2 minutes. Reduce the heat to low.

3. Add the broth, 1/2 cup at a time, stirring frequently until it is absorbed by the rice. Repeat the process for 20 to 30 minutes, until the rice is tender and all the broth has been added and absorbed.

4. Stir in the tomatoes and the Parmesan until they are completely incorporated. Stir in the butter to make the mixture creamy.

5. Season with salt and pepper. Garnish with the basil for adult servings. Serve immediately.

# salmon with couscous

This makes a quick, nutritious dinner for the entire family. Use a quick-cooking couscous to have dinner prepared in about 10 minutes.

**Serves 4**

GREEN ONIONS

1 bunch green onions, roots and ends trimmed

2 tablespoons extra virgin olive oil

Pinch of sea salt (optional)

SALMON

1/2 cup water

Juice of 1/2 lemon

1/4 cup unsalted butter

4 (6-ounce) salmon steaks

COUSCOUS

4 tablespoons butter

1 1/2 cups couscous

2 1/4 cups vegetable broth, warmed

1/2 teaspoon sea salt (optional)

1. Preheat the oven to 400°F. Rub a baking sheet with olive oil.

2. To prepare the green onions, brush the onions with the oil, place them on the baking sheet, and season with salt. Roast for about 5 minutes, until bright green and tender.

3. To prepare the salmon, in a medium sauté pan, bring the water and lemon juice to a boil. Add the butter and salmon steaks. Decrease the heat to medium and cover. Poach the steaks for about 8 minutes, and then turn them carefully to cook the other side. Remove from the heat and set aside.

4. To prepare the couscous, melt 3 tablespoons of the butter in a saucepan over medium heat. Add the couscous and stir until it is coated with the butter. Pour the vegetable broth into the couscous and add the salt. Bring the mixture to a boil, then decrease the heat to a simmer. Cover and cook for 5 to 7 minutes, until all the liquid is absorbed. Remove from the heat and stir in the remaining 1 tablespoon of butter. Cover and set aside.

5. To serve, place the couscous on a platter, arrange the salmon steaks on top, and lay the roasted green onions over the salmon steaks. Mash the salmon with the couscous for babies nine months to a year old and omit the onions.

# braised pork with apricots

This is best in apricot season with fresh apricots; otherwise, use organic dried apricots.

**Serves 6**

3 tablespoons extra virgin olive oil

2¹/₂ pounds boneless pork shoulder or butt roast

Sea salt and freshly ground black pepper (optional)

36 pearl onions, peeled

6 carrots, peeled and sliced into ¹/₂-inch pieces

1 bay leaf

1 tablespoon red wine vinegar

2 cups low-sodium chicken broth, plus more if necessary

12 fresh apricots, halved and pitted

1. Preheat the oven 375°F. Heat a Dutch oven over medium-high heat for 3 minutes. Add the oil. Add the pork and sear for 2 to 4 minutes, until brown on all sides, seasoning with salt and pepper as it is turned.

2. Remove the pork, pour off most of the rendered fat, and decrease the heat to medium-low. Add the onions and carrots and cook for 4 minutes. Add the bay leaf, vinegar, and 1 cup of the broth. Bring to a boil and boil for 1 minute.

3. Decrease the heat to low and return the meat to the pot. Pour in the remaining 1 cup of broth and bring to a boil. Remove from the heat, cover, and place in the oven for 45 minutes.

4. Return to the stove top and cook over low heat for about 45 minutes more. Add a little more broth, if necessary, so the vegetables don't dry out. When the meat and vegetables are tender, add the apricots and cook for 3 minutes over low heat.

5. Transfer the pork to a large bowl. Drain the vegetables and apricots, reserving the liquid, and place them in the bowl. In a saucepan over high heat, reduce the reserved liquid by half. Season with salt and pepper and return to the Dutch oven along with the meat and vegetables. Bring to a quick boil.

6. To serve, slice the pork and place each slice on a serving plate with some vegetables and apricots. Drizzle with the sauce.

# wild rice with mushrooms and onions

This is another variation on a risotto-style wild rice dish, this time with the pungent flavor of mushrooms and onions.

For babies nine to twelve months old, purée the rice mixture with enough chicken broth to reach the desired consistency.

**Serves 4 to 6**

4 cups low-sodium chicken broth

2 tablespoons extra virgin olive oil

1/4 cup minced sweet onion

1 cup 1/4-inch diced carrot

4 ounces shiitake, oyster, or button mushrooms, cleaned and cut into 1/4-inch pieces

1 1/2 cups wild rice, rinsed

1/2 cup grated Parmesan cheese

Leaves of 1 sprig fresh thyme

2 tablespoons unsalted butter, at room temperature

Sea salt and freshly ground black pepper

1. Heat the broth in a medium saucepan to a simmer over low heat.

2. In a large pot, heat the oil for 1 minute over medium-high heat. Add the onion, carrot, and mushrooms and cook for 6 to 8 minutes, until tender. Add the wild rice and stir for 1 minute to coat with the oil.

3. Pour 1/2 cup of the heated broth into the rice, stirring constantly. As the rice absorbs the broth, add additional broth in 1/2-cup increments. Repeat this process for 18 to 20 minutes, until the grains are tender and puffed. Remove the pan from the heat.

4. Add the Parmesan, thyme, and butter, stirring until creamy. Season with salt and pepper and serve immediately.

# biscuits

Biscuits are quick and versatile. They're great for breakfast with butter and jam, for dinner as an accompaniment to Chicken Pot Pie (page 53), or as dessert, smothered in fresh sliced strawberries with a dollop of whipped cream.

**Makes about 12 biscuits**

2 cups all-purpose flour

1 tablespoon baking soda

1 teaspoon sea salt

1/3 cup unsalted butter, plus additional melted butter for brushing tops

1 cup buttermilk

1. Preheat the oven to 350°F. Lightly grease a baking sheet with butter.

2. Combine the flour, baking soda, and salt in the bowl of a stand mixer fitted with the paddle attachment and mix on low speed. Add the 1/3 cup butter and mix until a very coarse meal forms. Add the buttermilk and continue to mix on low speed just to combine. Be careful not to overmix.

3. Turn the dough out onto a lightly floured work surface and pat out to about a 3/4-inch-think rectangle. Using a metal biscuit cutter or a glass, cut out 2-inch rounds. Press together the remaining dough and repeat the process to use it up. Place the biscuits about an inch apart on the baking sheet and brush the tops with melted butter.

4. Bake for 12 minutes, or until the tops are golden.

5. Let the biscuits cool briefly on a wire rack before serving.

# bran muffins

Muffins are a healthy alternative to cupcakes and cookies. Also, they can be baked ahead and frozen, which is perfect for a busy morning.

**Makes 18 regular or
36 mini muffins**

1/2 cup pecans, finely chopped

2 1/3 cups all-purpose flour

1 cup wheat bran

1 cup firmly packed light
    brown sugar

2 1/2 teaspoons baking soda

1/2 teaspoon baking powder

1/2 teaspoon sea salt

2 large eggs

1/2 cup canola oil

1 1/2 cups buttermilk

1/2 cup currants, finely chopped

1/2 cup cranberries, finely
    chopped

1. Preheat the oven to 425°F.

2. Arrange the pecans on a baking sheet in a single layer and toast for 6 to 8 minutes, turning over once, until browned and fragrant. When cool, chop finely.

3. Decrease the oven temperature to 375°F. Grease the cups of the muffin tins with canola oil; you can use either regular-size or mini muffin tins.

4. In a medium bowl, combine the flour, bran, sugar, baking soda, baking powder, and salt.

5. In a separate bowl, mix the eggs, oil, and buttermilk. Add the flour mixture and blend. Fold in the currants, cranberries, and pecans.

6. Use a small ice cream scoop or measure 2 tablespoons of batter into each of the regular muffin tins or about 1 tablespoon of batter into the mini. Bake on the center rack of the oven for about 20 minutes for the regular size or 15 minutes for the mini, until the tops are golden and a toothpick inserted into the center of one of the muffins comes out clean.

7. Let cool on a rack for about 5 minutes before serving warm. Put extras in a freezer bag (no plastic wrap), date them, freeze, and use them within a month.

# orange sable cookies

The orange zest adds a refreshing flavor to these cookies. We didn't start giving our boys cookies until they were about two, and then very seldom.

**Makes about 5 dozen**

4 cups all-purpose flour

1½ cups confectioners' sugar

Pinch of fine sea salt

3/4 cup unsalted butter

Zest of 2 oranges, finely minced

1 cup raw sugar, to coat

1. Sift together the flour, confectioners' sugar, and salt.

2. In the bowl of a stand mixer fitted with the paddle attachment, cream the butter on high speed for about 3 minutes, until light and fluffy. Add the orange zest and beat on low speed for 1 minute. With the mixer on low speed, add the flour mixture, pausing to scrape down the sides of the bowl. Continue to beat just until the dough is smooth. Be careful not to overbeat.

3. Divide the dough into three equal portions. Roll each into a log about 1 1/2 inches thick and 5 inches long. Pour the raw sugar onto a baking sheet and roll the logs in it to coat evenly. Wrap each log in plastic wrap. Refrigerate for 1 hour. (The logs may be frozen for up to 2 weeks. If frozen, defrost in the refrigerator overnight to use.)

4. Preheat the oven to 375°F. Line a baking sheet with parchment paper.

5. Cut the dough into 3/8-inch-thick slices and place on the baking sheet.

6. Bake for 8 to 10 minutes, until the edges turn light golden brown. Transfer to a rack to cool.

# apple apricot compote

Fresh apricots are really necessary for the success of this compote. Dried apricots make the texture too chewy.

**Serves 4**

1 cup water

1 teaspoon freshly squeezed lemon juice

1/4 cup sugar

2 Braeburn, Cortland, or Jonagold apples, peeled, cored, and cut into 1/2-inch pieces

8 fresh apricots, pitted and cut into 1/2-inch pieces

1 strip lemon zest, for garnish (optional)

1. In a medium saucepan, combine the water, lemon juice, and sugar over medium heat and cook, swirling the pan occasionally, for 3 to 4 minutes, until the sugar dissolves.

2. Add the apples and cook for 6 to 8 minutes, until the apples are tender but not soft. Add the apricots and cook until just tender, about 2 minutes.

3. Serve warm or at room temperature garnished with a strip of lemon zest.

# 5 family feasts

Holiday meals are the events that punctuate the year, mark the changes of seasons, remind us what life should be about. In our house these are sprawling family affairs with relatives and friends and their kids. Kids are a vital part of the affair; they put us on our best behavior and reconnect us to our youth.

Most of the dishes in the following menus can be adjusted easily for babies as young as six months. Until they are about eighteen months, they will probably eat only a small portion of one or two dishes.

# Thanksgiving

**super mashed potatoes** | 91

**pumpkin risotto** | 93

**caramel cranberry sauce** | 94

Thanksgiving is our favorite holiday. It's a harvest feast, where the bounty of the season is celebrated at the table with friends and family. And it doesn't involve frenzied gift shopping.

# super mashed potatoes

This is one of my signature dishes and a holiday dish that almost the whole family can enjoy, but it's too rich for babies younger than nine months old.

**Serves 10 to 12**

4 pounds Yukon gold potatoes, peeled and quartered

2 cups milk or cream, heated

10 tablespoons unsalted butter, cut into cubes, at room temperature

1/2 cup plain yogurt

Salt and freshly ground black pepper

1. In a large, heavy-bottomed saucepan, bring lightly salted water to a boil and carefully drop in the potatoes. Decrease the heat and cook for about 30 minutes, until the potatoes are tender and easily pierced with the tip of a knife.

2. Drain immediately and press the potatoes through a potato ricer.

3. Return the riced potatoes to the saucepan. Beat in the milk until smooth. Add the butter and beat until completely melted. Over low heat, stir in the yogurt.

4. Season with salt and pepper. Serve warm.

# pumpkin risotto

Risotto makes an unusual but tasty stuffing, especially when made with pumpkin. The risotto complements the Thanksgiving turkey and is a refreshing change from having pumpkin in its traditional role as pie. Use canned pumpkin purée only as a last resort.

For babies nine to twelve months old, remove about 1/2 cup of the risotto from the pan before seasoning and adding the cheese. Mash it with a little chicken broth. If serving with turkey, make sure that the meat is cut into small enough pieces and serve only to children a year and older.

**Serves 4 to 6**

1 (1-pound) fresh pumpkin, peeled, seeded, and cut into 1-inch cubes, or 1 1/3 cups canned, unsweetened pumpkin purée

7 1/2 cups low-sodium chicken broth

10 tablespoons unsalted butter, at room temperature

1/3 cup finely minced onion

1 cup small button mushrooms

2 cups Arborio rice

1 1/2 teaspoons finely minced fresh sage

Sea salt and freshly ground black pepper

1/2 cup freshly grated Parmesan cheese

1. In a large covered pan, boil the fresh pumpkin in 1 cup lightly salted water for about 10 minutes, until the pumpkin is tender and can be pierced easily with the tip of a knife. Transfer the pumpkin with 1/2 cup of its cooking liquid to a blender or food processor fitted with a steel blade and purée. Set aside. If you are using canned pumpkin purée, omit this step.

2. Bring the chicken broth to a steady simmer in a large saucepan.

3. In a large heavy-bottomed pan over medium heat, melt 4 tablespoons of the butter. Add the onion and cook for 6 to 8 minutes, until translucent. Add the mushrooms and cook for 3 minutes. Add the rice and, using a wooden spoon, stir for 1 to 2 minutes, until all the grains are coated. Add the broth 1/2 cup at a time, stirring frequently. When the rice has almost absorbed the broth, add the next 1/2 cup. Continue adding more broth and stirring, reserving 1/2 cup of broth for the finish.

continued

4. When the rice is tender but still firm and 7 cups of the broth has been added and absorbed, mix in the reserved 1/2 cup broth, the pumpkin purée, sage, and salt and pepper. Add the cheese and the remaining 6 tablespoons of butter. Remove from the heat and cover to keep warm.

# caramel cranberry sauce

Deglazing with cream lightens the texture of the sauce.

Mash this well for babies nine months to three years old; whole berries can present a choking hazard for children under three.

**Makes 4 cups**

2 cups granulated sugar

2/3 cup water

2/3 cup heavy whipping cream

2 pounds fresh cranberries, washed, dried, and any bad berries discarded

Zest of 2 lemons, cut into strips

1. Combine the sugar and water in a heavy-bottomed saucepan. Dissolve the sugar in the water over medium heat until the liquid is completely clear. Increase the heat to high and cook (without stirring) until the caramel is a golden amber color.

2. Remove the caramel from the heat and slowly whisk in the cream, a few tablespoons at a time. The mixture will bubble as you add the cream.

3. Add the cranberries to the caramel and cook over low heat until tender. Stir in the lemon zest. Serve at room temperature.

# Christmas

**popovers** | 97

**butternut squash soup** | 99

**mashed turnips** | 100

**creamed cipollini onions and spinach** | 101

**roasted root vegetables** | 103

In the kitchen we pull out all the stops
for Christmas. This is a true feast and even
when the boys were very little they knew
something special was going on.

# popovers

Popovers make a good accompaniment to English-style dishes like roast beef. Tear the popovers into little pieces for babies one to two years old.

**Makes about 1 dozen**

1 cup all-purpose flour

1/4 teaspoon sea salt

1 cup whole milk

3 large eggs

1 tablespoon unsalted butter,
    melted

Pinch of fresh thyme

1. Preheat the oven to 450°F. Grease a popover tin or a muffin tin with melted butter and place in the oven to heat.

2. In a medium bowl, combine the flour and salt.

3. In a separate bowl, whisk together the milk, eggs, and butter. Pour into the flour mixture. Add the thyme and whisk until just blended.

4. Remove the heated pan from the oven and carefully fill each cup halfway with the batter. Place in the oven and lower the heat to 350°F. Bake for 15 to 20 minutes. The tops should be browned, but don't open the oven to check until they have baked for at least 15 minutes. They fall easily.

5. Serve hot from the oven.

# butternut squash soup

The savory-sweet flavor of the squash makes this soup a holiday favorite.

For babies six months to one year old, purée some of the cooked flesh from the squash moistened with chicken stock. For adults at the table, serve with a crostini topped with wild mushrooms.

**Serves 6**

3 pounds butternut squash, halved and seeded

6 to 7 tablespoons unsalted butter

Sea salt and freshly ground black pepper

1 large onion, finely chopped

1 large carrot, peeled and cut into 1/2-inch slices

2 celery stalks, trimmed and cut into 1/2-inch slices

1 cup low-sodium chicken broth, plus extra for purée

1. Preheat the oven to 375°F.

2. Place the squash halves on a baking sheet cut side up. Place 1 tablespoon of butter in each cavity and season with salt and pepper. Cover the pan with aluminum foil and roast for 30 to 45 minutes, until the squash is tender and easily pierced with the tip of a knife. Remove from the oven and set aside to cool. Leave the oven on.

3. In a large pot, melt the remaining 4 tablespoons of butter over medium-high heat. Add the onion, carrot, and celery and sauté for about 5 minutes. Add the broth and cook over medium heat for about 10 minutes more, until the vegetables are tender. Remove the pan from the heat and let cool. Transfer the mixture to a food processor fitted with a steel blade and purée until smooth.

4. Scrape the flesh from the squash and add to the food processor. Purée until smooth, adding more broth as needed. Taste and adjust seasonings.

5. To serve, reheat the soup until just bubbling and pour into individual bowls. For babies, test the temperature before serving.

# mashed turnips

Turnips have a sweet, delicate flavor and can be used as a good alternative to mashed potatoes. Choose white or purple-tinged ones, no larger than 2 inches in diameter.

Mashed turnips can be served to babies nine months and older.

**Serves 6**

3 pounds turnips, peeled and cut into chunks

3 tablespoons unsalted butter, at room temperature

1/2 cup whole milk, heated

Sea salt and freshly ground black pepper

1. Bring a large pot of lightly salted water to a boil. Add the turnips and cook for 15 to 20 minutes, until tender. Drain.

2. Combine the turnips with the butter and milk in a food processor fitted with a steel blade, and purée.

3. Season with salt and pepper and serve.

# creamed cipollini onions and spinach

This little onion, actually a bulb of the grape hyacinth, can be found in Italian and specialty markets in the fall.

For babies eighteen months and older, purée or mash with the liquid, depending on your baby's ability to chew.

**Serves 6**

1/4 cup extra virgin olive oil

1 1/2 pounds cipollini onions, peeled

8 ounces spinach, rinsed and stemmed

1/2 cup heavy cream

Sea salt and freshly ground black pepper

1. In a large heavy pan, heat the oil over medium heat for 1 minute. Add the onions, cover, and cook for 20 to 30 minutes, until tender.

2. In a large sauté pan over medium-high heat, cook the spinach with just the water that clings to its leaves for 2 to 3 minutes, until it is bright green and tender. Refresh the spinach in iced water. When cool, drain it and remove the excess water by squeezing it with your hands.

3. When the onions are tender, decrease the heat to medium, add the cream, and cook for 1 to 2 minutes, until bubbling. Add the spinach and cook for 2 to 3 minutes, until it's warm and the sauce has thickened slightly.

4. Season with salt and pepper and serve.

# roasted root vegetables

Scarlet beets and orange carrots make this an attractive dish for a holiday table, and it's the ideal winter comfort food.

    The nitrates in some root vegetables, especially beets, make this unsuitable for babies younger than nine months. For babies nine to eighteen months old, pick out the parsnips, rutabagas, and carrots, and purée with a little liquid. For older babies, chop into smaller pieces.

**Serves 6**

2 celery roots, peeled and cut into large dice

3 parsnips, peeled and cut into large dice

3 rutabagas, peeled and cut into large dice

6 carrots, peeled and cut into large dice

3 onions, cut into large dice

Extra virgin olive oil, for coating

Sea salt and freshly ground black pepper

6 cloves garlic, minced

Leaves of 1 sprig fresh thyme

6 red beets, peeled and cut into large dice

1 tablespoon aged balsamic vinegar

1. Preheat the oven to 375°F.

2. Combine the celery roots, parsnips, rutabagas, carrots, and onions in a large shallow roasting pan. Coat with olive oil, salt, pepper, garlic, and some of the thyme. Roast for 45 to 55 minutes, until the vegetables are tender and easily pierced with the tip of a knife.

3. Coat the beets with olive oil, salt, pepper, and the remaining thyme, and roast in a separate pan but at the same time as the other vegetables for about 45 minutes, until tender. Put both pans on the middle rack if they will fit. If not, use the racks just above and below the middle, and switch positions after about 35 minutes.

4. Remove the pans from the oven and mix the beets into the other vegetables. Return to the oven and roast for another 5 minutes.

5. Toss with the balsamic vinegar. Season with salt and pepper. Serve immediately.

# Easter

**roasted herbed potatoes** | **105**

**asparagus and eight-minute egg** | **107**

**panna cotta with strawberries** | **108**

Easter signals that nature is waking up and soon
we'll have fresh spring produce. We celebrate
Easter in a traditional manner, with a boisterous
Easter egg hunt and lamb for dinner.

# roasted herbed potatoes

For babies nine months to one year old, purée a few slices of potato with a little water; mash or cut them into small pieces for toddlers.

**Serves 6**

3 pounds new potatoes, halved lengthwise

1/4 cup extra virgin olive oil

1 clove garlic, minced

1 tablespoon fresh rosemary

Sea salt and freshly ground black pepper

Pinch of fresh thyme leaves

1 tablespoon minced fresh oregano leaves

1. Preheat the oven to 350°F.

2. Arrange the potatoes in a single layer in a large ovenproof baking dish and toss to coat with the oil, garlic, and rosemary. Season with salt and pepper.

3. Roast, uncovered, for 20 to 25 minutes. Remove the pan from the oven and add the thyme and oregano, turning the potatoes with a wooden spatula. Continue roasting for another 10 minutes, until the potatoes are tender and easily pierced with the tip of a knife.

4. Serve immediately or at room temperature.

# asparagus and eight-minute egg

Choose very fresh asparagus, similar in size so that they cook at the same rate.

The hard-cooked egg yolk can be puréed with some asparagus and enough water or chicken broth to make it smooth for babies nine months to one year old. For babies one year and older, mash the asparagus with both the yolk and the egg white.

**Serves 6**

36 medium to large stalks asparagus, ends trimmed

6 large eggs

CHAMPAGNE VINAIGRETTE

1½ tablespoons champagne vinegar

Pinch of sea salt

1 cup extra virgin olive oil

1 tablespoon minced shallot

Freshly ground black pepper

1 bunch chives, minced, for garnish (optional)

1. Bring a large pan of salted water to a boil, add the asparagus, and blanch for 5 to 7 minutes, until just tender. Drain and immediately refresh in ice water. When the asparagus is cool, drain and set aside.

2. Pierce the eggs with a pin at the wide end and place in a medium saucepan with boiling water over high heat. Cook them for 8 minutes. Place in a bowl of cold water to cool.

3. To prepare the champagne vinaigrette, whisk the vinegar, salt, oil, shallot, and pepper in a small bowl.

4. On a cutting board, line up the asparagus at the tips and cut the stalks to the same length. Chop the stalks into smaller pieces for children three years and older.

5. To serve, arrange the asparagus on individual serving plates or a platter. Shell the eggs, cut into medium dice, and scatter over the asparagus. Drizzle 2 to 3 tablespoons of the vinaigrette over each serving. Sprinkle with chives.

# panna cotta with strawberries

A good balsamic vinegar, aged ten years or more, will boost the flavor of the strawberries and provide a satisfying contrast with the smooth sweetness of the "cooked cream."

Everyone over the age of one can eat this. Purée or mash the berries without the vinegar for children younger than three years old.

**Serves 8**

3 cups heavy cream

1 cup whole milk

2 cups confectioners' sugar

1 vanilla bean

3 sheets leaf gelatin

1½ pounds strawberries, hulled and halved

5 tablespoons granulated sugar

5 teaspoons aged balsamic vinegar

1. In a large saucepan, combine the cream, milk, and confectioners' sugar. Slice the vanilla bean open lengthwise, scrape out the seeds, and add both the seeds and the pod to the cream mixture. Mix and bring to a boil over medium-high heat. Decrease the heat and simmer for about 7 minutes.

2. Remove the pan from the heat and add the gelatin, stirring with a wooden spoon until dissolved.

3. Remove the vanilla bean and strain the mixture through a fine-mesh sieve. Pour into individual serving dishes and chill for at least 3 hours.

4. In a bowl, mix the strawberries, granulated sugar, and vinegar, making sure the berries are completely coated. Let marinate for 30 minutes, stirring occasionally.

5. Serve the panna cotta chilled and pass the strawberries on the side.

# Passover

**matzo ball soup** | **110**

**spinach with pine nuts** | **113**

**flourless chocolate hazelnut cake** | **114**

Although Passover meals are prepared
according to strict dietary guidelines,
that doesn't prevent the dishes from being
delicious for the entire family.

# matzo ball soup

We all need bowls of chicken soup sometimes. The chicken used in preparation can be used later for Chicken Pot Pie (page 53). Purée the matzo ball and soup for children one to three years old.

**Serves 8**

CHICKEN SOUP

1 (4-pound) whole chicken

3 celery stalks, cut into 3-inch pieces

2 large onions, quartered

3 carrots, peeled and cut into 3-inch pieces

Bouquet garni (3 sprigs each of thyme, rosemary, marjoram, and oregano tied with kitchen twine)

4 cloves garlic

MATZO BALLS

2 cups finely ground matzo meal

4 large eggs, slightly beaten

1 teaspoon kosher salt

2 tablespoons club soda

1/4 cup vegetable oil

2 teaspoons finely minced flat-leaf parsley

1. To prepare the soup, rinse the chicken under cold water and pat dry with paper towels.

2. Combine the chicken, celery, onions, carrots, bouquet garni, and garlic in a heavy-bottomed pot with water to cover. Bring to a boil. Decrease the heat, cover, and cook for 1 hour, or until the juices run clear when the chicken is pierced in the thigh with a knife. Remove the chicken and set aside to cool. Strain the broth, discarding the vegetables, and skim off any excess fat. Strain the broth once more through a fine-mesh sieve and return to the pot.

3. While the soup is cooking, prepare the matzo balls. Thoroughly mix the matzo meal and eggs. Add the salt, club soda, oil, and parsley. Refrigerate for at least 30 minutes or overnight.

4. Warm the broth over medium heat for about 10 minutes before adding the matzo balls.

5. With your hands, form the matzo mixture into balls about 2 inches in diameter and place in the heated broth. Cook for about 40 minutes over medium heat, until tender.

6. Serve immediately.

# spinach with pine nuts

Purée the sautéed spinach without the pine nuts and before you have seasoned it for babies nine to eighteen months; chop it into small pieces for toddlers up to three years. Children two and older may also have pine nuts. If there is a family history of allergies to nuts, wait until your child is three to introduce them.

**Serves 8**

½ cup pine nuts

5 tablespoons extra virgin olive oil

1 clove garlic, minced

1 shallot, minced

3 pounds spinach, washed and stemmed

1 tablespoon freshly squeezed lemon juice

Pinch of ground nutmeg

Sea salt and freshly ground black pepper

1. Preheat the oven to 350°F.

2. Spread the pine nuts on a baking sheet and toast for 3 to 5 minutes, until lightly browned. Watch closely; they go from toasted to burned in a matter of seconds.

3. In a large sauté pan, heat 2 tablespoons of the oil over medium-high heat for 1 minute. Add the garlic and shallot and sauté for 1 minute. Add the spinach and sauté, turning constantly, for 1 minute, until wilted. Add the pine nuts, the remaining 3 tablespoons of oil, and the lemon juice, tossing constantly for 1 minute. Season with the nutmeg and salt and pepper.

4. Transfer immediately to a serving dish and serve.

# flourless chocolate hazelnut cake

Serve this warm with a dollop of crème fraîche.

Even though we love this cake and are tempted to offer them a taste, babies are not ready to handle chocolate until they are over two years old. If there is a family history of allergies to nuts, wait until your child is three to introduce them.

**Serves 12**

2 cups hazelnuts

12 ounces semisweet chocolate chips

1¼ cups unsalted butter

8 eggs, separated

2⅓ cups confectioners' sugar, plus extra for dusting

Pinch of sea salt

1. Preheat the oven to 375°F. Lightly grease a 10-inch springform pan and line with parchment paper.

2. In a food processor, grind the hazelnuts into small pieces.

3. Combine the chocolate and butter in a heatproof bowl over a pot of simmering water. Make sure the base of the bowl doesn't touch the water. Stir occasionally until the butter and chocolate have melted. Set aside to cool.

4. While the chocolate is melting, beat the egg yolks with a whisk.

5. Transfer the chocolate mixture to the bowl of a stand mixer fitted with the paddle attachment. On low speed, slowly add the egg yolks. Stir in the hazelnuts.

6. Sift the confectioners' sugar into a bowl and add to the chocolate mixture. The mixture will be stiff.

7. In a separate bowl of the mixer, using the whisk attachment, beat the egg whites and salt on high speed until stiff peaks form.

8. Carefully fold one-third of the egg whites into the chocolate mixture with a large rubber spatula. Repeat this process until all the egg whites have been folded in.

9. Pour the mixture into the prepared cake pan and bake for 45 minutes. The cake is done when a toothpick inserted into the center comes out with a light coating. The cake will be moist.

10. Transfer the cake to a cooling rack and let it sit for 20 minutes. Remove from the springform pan, and place on a rack to cool completely.

11. Just before serving, sift confectioner's sugar over the top of the cake.

# Fourth of July

**corn and tomato bread** | **117**

**baked beans with apple-smoked bacon** | **118**

**roasted potato slices** | **120**

The Fourth is another holiday that is really
all about family, friends, and food, and it's during
summer, when most produce is at its peak.

# corn and tomato bread

Chunks of roasted tomato—and whole corn kernels in the adult version—add a little surprise and texture to the usual suspect.

Since whole corn kernels can be a choking hazard, we've left them out of the main recipe. For adults and older children, shuck and boil 3 large ears of fresh corn, scrape the kernels off the cob, and fold into the batter when adding the tomatoes.

**Serves 8**

1³/4 cups yellow cornmeal

1 cup all-purpose flour

1/2 cup sugar

1 teaspoon baking powder

1 teaspoon sea salt

1 teaspoon baking soda

1 large egg

2¹/4 cups buttermilk

1/4 cup diced and drained
    fire-roasted tomatoes

1. Preheat the oven to 400°F. Lightly coat an 8-inch square baking pan with canola oil.

2. Mix the cornmeal, flour, sugar, baking powder, salt, and baking soda in a medium bowl.

3. In the bowl of a stand mixer with the whisk attachment, mix together the egg and buttermilk at medium speed. Replace the whisk with the paddle attachment and add the flour mixture. Mix on medium speed. Fold in the tomatoes with a large spatula.

4. Set the prepared pan in the oven until it begins to smoke. Remove and pour in the batter. Bake for about 35 minutes, until golden brown; a toothpick inserted into the center should come out clean. Let the bread cool in the pan for 20 minutes, then remove it and cut it into 8 pieces.

# baked beans with apple-smoked bacon

The crunchy bacon crust is reason alone to make this baked bean dish, especially if it's made with apple-smoked bacon, which you can find in most markets.

For babies nine to twelve months old, purée the beans in a food processor fitted with a steel blade with enough chicken broth to achieve the desired consistency.

**Serves 8**

2 pounds navy or other white beans, rinsed and picked over

1 pound apple-smoked bacon, cut into thin strips, plus 10 whole strips

1/2 sweet onion, finely chopped

1 cup pure maple syrup

1 cup dark molasses

2 teaspoons Dijon mustard

1 cup low-sodium chicken broth (optional)

Sea salt and freshly ground black pepper

Dried breadcrumbs

1. Cover the beans with cold water and soak overnight. Rinse, drain, and set aside.

2. In a large ovenproof casserole over medium-high heat, cook the sliced bacon strips for about 3 minutes, until the fat is translucent. Add the onion and cook for about 5 minutes, until it is soft, stirring occasionally with a wooden spoon.

3. Add the beans and coat well with the bacon and onion mixture. Cover with 1 inch of water, cover, and cook over medium-high heat for 1 hour, stirring occasionally.

4. Preheat the oven to 350°F.

5. Add the syrup, molasses, and mustard to the beans and mix well. Place the casserole in the oven, covered, and bake for about 2 hours, until the beans are tender. Check occasionally to make sure the beans aren't dry. Stir in the 1 cup chicken broth if necessary to maintain a creamy consistency. When the beans are tender, remove from the oven and mix, bringing the bacon up from the bottom. Season with salt and pepper.

6. Partially cook the whole bacon strips in a large sauté pan for about 3 minutes, until the fat is translucent. Remove and drain on paper towels. Place the strips on top of the beans and cover with a thin layer of breadcrumbs.

7. Turn the oven up to 400°F. Return the casserole to the oven and bake, uncovered, for about 5 minutes, until the breadcrumbs are browned and the beans are bubbling.

8. Serve warm directly out of the casserole.

# roasted potato slices

Instead of potato salad, I like to serve crunchy roasted Yukon gold potato slices. Choose potatoes that are roughly equal in size so that the slices make an attractive pattern when you overlap them on the serving dish.

Remove a few potato slices before brushing with the vinaigrette and purée with some water to the desired consistency for babies six to nine months old; mash them into bite-size lumps for babies nine months to two years old.

**Serves 8**

3 pounds medium Yukon gold potatoes, cut lengthwise into 1/2-inch-thick slices (do not peel)

6 tablespoons extra virgin olive oil

Sea salt and freshly ground black pepper

BALSAMIC VINAIGRETTE

1 1/2 tablespoons balsamic vinegar

6 tablespoons extra virgin olive oil

1 teaspoon Dijon mustard

Fresh thyme leaves

Fresh rosemary sprigs, for garnish

1. Preheat the oven to 350°F.

2. Coat the potato slices generously with the oil. Season with salt and pepper.

3. Arrange the slices in a single layer on a baking sheet and cover tightly with aluminum foil. Roast for about 15 minutes. Turn the slices over and roast, uncovered, for 10 to 12 minutes, until golden brown.

4. To prepare the vinaigrette, while the potatoes are roasting, whisk together the vinegar, oil, and mustard.

5. To serve, place the slices in an overlapping pattern on a large platter and brush with the vinaigrette. Sprinkle with thyme leaves and garnish with a couple sprigs of rosemary.

# recommended reading

Atkinson, Catherine. *Real Food for Your Baby.* London: Foulsham & Co., Ltd., 2001.

Charlton, Carol. *Family Organic Cookbook.* Newton Abbot, UK: Charles & David, 2000.

Kalnins, Diana, & Joanne Saab. *Better Baby Food.* Toronto: Robert Rose, Inc., 2001.

Kimmel, Martha, & David Kimmel, with Suzanne Goldenson. *Mommy Made and Daddy Too! Home Cooking for a Healthy Baby & Toddler.* New York: Bantam Books, 2000.

Lewis, Sara. *First Food: Preparing Food for Babies and Toddlers.* Bath, UK: Southwater, 2000.

Satter, Ellyn. *Child of Mine: Feeding with Love and Good Sense.* 3rd edition. Palo Alto: Bull Publishing Company, 2000.

Sweet, Robin O., & Thomas A. Bloom. *The Well Fed Baby: Healthy, Delicious Baby Food Recipes That You Can Make at Home.* New York: William Morrow, 2000.

Vann, Lizzie. *Organic Baby & Toddler Cookbook: Easy Recipes for Natural Food.* New York: Dorling Kindersley Publishing, Inc., 2001.

# metric conversions

## LIQUID WEIGHT

| U.S. Measurement | Metric Equivalent |
|---|---|
| 1/4 teaspoon | 1.23 ml |
| 1/2 teaspoon | 2.5 ml |
| 3/4 teaspoon | 3.7 ml |
| 1 teaspoon | 5 ml |
| 1 dessert spoon | 10 ml |
| 1 tablespoon (3 teaspoons) | 15 ml |
| 2 tablespoons (1 ounce) | 30 ml |
| 1/4 cup | 60 ml |
| 1/3 cup | 80 ml |
| 1/2 cup | 120 ml |
| 2/3 cup | 160 ml |
| 3/4 cup | 180 ml |
| 1 cup (8 ounces) | 240 ml |
| 2 cups (1 pint) | 480 ml |
| 3 cups | 720 ml |
| 4 cups (1 quart) | 1 liter |
| 4 quarts (1 gallon) | 3 3/4 liters |

## DRY WEIGHT

| U.S. Measurement | Metric Equivalent |
|---|---|
| 1/4 ounce | 7 grams |
| 1/3 ounce | 10 grams |
| 1/2 ounce | 14 grams |
| 1 ounce | 28 grams |
| 1 1/2 ounces | 42 grams |
| 1 3/4 ounces | 50 grams |
| 2 ounces | 57 grams |
| 3 ounces | 85 grams |
| 3 1/2 ounces | 100 grams |
| 4 ounces (1/4 pound) | 114 grams |
| 6 ounces | 170 grams |
| 8 ounces (1/2 pound) | 227 grams |
| 9 ounces | 250 grams |
| 16 ounces (1 pound) | 464 grams |
| 1.1 pounds | 500 grams |
| 2.2 pounds | 1,000 grams |

## TEMPERATURES

| Fahrenheit | Celsius (Centigrade) |
|---|---|
| 32°F (water freezes) | 0°C |
| 200°F | 95°C |
| 212°F (water boils) | 100°C |
| 225°F | 110°C |
| 250°F | 120°C |
| 275°F | 135°C |
| 300°F (slow oven) | 150°C |
| 325°F | 160°C |
| 350°F (moderate oven) | 175°C |
| 375°F | 190°C |
| 400°F (hot oven) | 205°C |
| 425°F | 220°C |
| 450°F (very hot oven) | 230°C |
| 475°F | 245°C |
| 500°F (extremely hot oven) | 260°C |

## LENGTH

| U.S. Measurement | Metric Equivalent |
|---|---|
| 1/8 inch | 3 mm |
| 1/4 inch | 6 mm |
| 3/8 inch | 1 cm |
| 1/2 inch | 12 mm |
| 3/4 inch | 2 cm |
| 1 inch | 2.5 cm |
| 2 inches | 5 cm |
| 3 inches | 7.5 cm |
| 4 inches | 10 cm |
| 5 inches | 12.5 cm |

## APPROXIMATE EQUIVALENTS

| |
|---|
| 1 kilo is slightly more than 2 pounds |
| 1 liter is slightly more than 1 quart |
| 1 deciliter is slightly less than 1/2 cup |
| 1 meter is slightly more than 3 feet |
| 1 centiliter is approximately 2 teaspoons |
| 1 centimeter is approximately 3/8 inch |

# index